LEARNING BEHAVIOURS

A PRACTICAL GUIDE TO SELF-REGULATION IN THE EARLY YEARS

SUE COWLEY

JOHN CATT

First Published 2021

by John Catt Educational Ltd,
15 Riduna Park, Station Road,
Melton, Woodbridge IP12 1QT

Tel: +44 (0) 1394 389850
Email: enquiries@johncatt.com
Website: www.johncatt.com

ISBN: 978 1 913622 39 8

Set and designed by John Catt Educational Limited

Reviews

This book is a 'must read' for everyone in early years. It guides the reader through the importance of tuning in to young children's behaviour as a form of communication to be responded to with co-regulation, rather than annoyances to be 'dealt' with by discipline. Sue's clear writing effectively explains the relationship of self-regulation to learning about appropriate behaviours and provides lots of practical ideas for turning settings into learning communities where everyone's behaviour supports emotional and cognitive self-regulation.

Helen Moylett, Early Years Consultant and Writer

This book is packed with clear guidance and practical advice for anyone working with young children. Starting with the concept that for our youngest children behaviour is a form of communication, from babies' cries to throwing toys in frustration, Sue helps practitioners consider how to tune in to the child and their needs, in order to support, co-regulate with the child and guide them to manage and deal with a wide range of emotions.

The four overarching principles of the English Early Years Foundation Stage shine through in every chapter. A clear understanding of the unique child, developing in different ways and at different rates in an enabling environment through positive relationships is demonstrated throughout. The focus on really tuning in to children's needs, which is so fundamental to early development, is refreshing. Many behaviour approaches applied to EYFS are often very similar to approaches used in primary and secondary schools and don't always recognise the unique needs of the young child. Expecting a child to be able to self–regulate when they may not actually understand or be able to name or express their feelings is neither desirable nor wholly successful. In order to be able to self-regulate, young children need to understand their emotions, and that they can have some control over their responses to them. Sue provides a range of accessible ideas to support practitioners with this important area of emotional regulation.

This isn't just a book about behaviour, though, as with all things in Early Years, the holistic approach covers all aspects of working with young children. Chapters on developing enabling environments to support independence and self-regulation, and on the potential pros and cons of different approaches to curriculum, will provide anyone with an interest in how young children learn with some thought-provoking ideas to explore in order to shape their thinking. A range of case studies provides practical support to practitioners encountering most commonly experienced, specific issues for the first time. I would recommend this as a must-read for anyone working with children under the age of seven.

Ruth Swailes, Improvement Adviser and Education Consultant

I enjoyed reading this new book by Sue Cowley, *Learning behaviours: a practical guide to self-regulation in the Early Years*. For many years I have championed the need for more understanding of self-regulation within Early Years. I am delighted that Sue has written this book for the sector.

I love that it is written in an easy-to-read format. I especially appreciate how Sue has explained how the educator can become a 'child whisperer'; what I call being turned on and tuned in to children, physically and emotionally.

I would recommend that every setting has a copy of this book and that educators read it so they can discuss, reflect and update their practice with the child at the centre.

Laura Henry-Allain, International speaker, writer (creator of the JoJo and Gran Gran characters) and consultant

Acknowledgements

A huge 'thank you' to my Firm Foundations friends for everything they have taught me about early years and for just being generally lovely – Nicky Clements, Simona McKenzie, Claire Navaie, Ruth Swailes, Kate Thompson and Helen Williams.

Thanks to the team at John Catt.

Thanks to my family for their continued support.

And special thanks to all the staff, children, parents, families and committee members at Stanton Drew and Pensford Preschool.

This book is dedicated to Lynne Willmott – thanks
for having me along for the ride!

Contents

Introduction

The period from birth to five years old is a crucial time in a child's development. Their brains and bodies go through a period of very rapid development as they explore their world, build their physical strength, develop language and gain the social and emotional skills that they need to be happy and successful. This is a rate of change that will never be matched again. It is at this crucial time that the foundations for behaviour are being laid – it is a time when our babies, toddlers and young children are literally *learning behaviours*. The purpose of this book is to help you find out more about how behaviour is learned in the early years, and to give you lots of practical advice about supporting children to build their skills in self-regulation.

From the moment we are born, we are learning how to behave within the world we inhabit. At first our worlds are small – a handful of close family members. But as we grow and develop, we must make our way through a world that is frequently puzzling, challenging and difficult to navigate, although equally one that is often full of joy, wonder and warmth. Learning the appropriate behaviours to fit into and succeed within our world is a key part of developing through childhood, adolescence and into adulthood. Gradually, we understand which behaviours are okay and which ones are not. We learn over time to manage our impulses and to deal with the things that we find difficult. In a similar way to how we learn subjects in a classroom, so we learn behaviours too: we need adults to support us in modelling, discussing, thinking, questioning and practising them. Rather than hoping that a system or a policy can do all or most of the work for us in getting children to behave, it is helpful to see behaviour as simply another part of the learning process.

The learning of behaviours does not begin when a child arrives in an early years setting – the process starts from the very first interactions with parents or carers. It is these first years that form the basis for what happens later on. The modelling, support and teaching of behaviours by parents and early years practitioners is critical in laying firm foundations for children's future behaviour and learning. We need to support the learning of the 'how to' of behaviour – developing all aspects of self-regulation such as impulse control, dealing with challenges, focusing attention, and so on. We also need to support the learning of the 'why to' of behaviour – helping children understand how what they do impacts on others and why it is important to 'behave well' in different contexts. In this book I explore the practicalities of doing this with children in an early years setting. The advice and strategies in this book are designed to help you, whether you work as a childminder or in a day-care nursery, a preschool, an independent school, a maintained nursery school or a school reception class. This book may also be useful for parents/carers and for teachers working with older children, to learn more about how these skills develop.

Children in the early years are right at the start of their journey towards learning behaviours – they are still young and prone to impulsive behaviours – their biology and lack of physical independence mitigates against them behaving in the same way as adults do. They have not yet mastered what we refer to as 'self-regulation'. When babies or toddlers are tired or hungry, they cry to gain our attention – young children are dependent on the adults around them to ensure that their needs are met. In early years settings, we work with and alongside our families to support children in learning the behaviours that will help them to both learn while they are with us and thrive within society. This is one of the most important lessons that children learn during their education – that they have the power within themselves to regulate their own responses, impulses, behaviours and learning.

The skills that children need to acquire in order to behave in the appropriate way for learning are complex and varied. They must learn self-regulation in all its forms: how to stay calm, how to have empathy, how to be kind, how to cooperate, how to share, how to take turns, how to focus, how to be responsible, how to be independent, how to make good choices, and so on. Learning these behaviours is critical, not only for academic success, but also for creating a better and more equitable society. The hope is that, when our learners leave our early years settings and move on to the next phase in their education, the behaviours we have helped them to learn will put them in the best position to succeed and to work in a cooperative way with their peers and teachers. Although systems, policies and processes can be useful and effective in managing behaviour, this book will help you examine your assumptions about 'what works' and how you can support your children in learning to behave.

In this book I explore and examine a set of principles around behaviour that will help you to support young children in learning and developing while they are in your care. The principles explained and described in this book will help you understand more about why young children behave as they do, and what you can do about it to support them better. I also include some points for reflection, for practitioners to use with their staff teams, and a series of case studies to show you how you might approach and deal with some the commonest kinds of problematic behaviours that you see in young children. Above all else, this book contains practical advice and hands-on strategies that you can put into place in your setting immediately. Although there is no 'magic wand' that will allow you to 'solve' all the behaviour issues you might face, there is lots you can do to support your children, to help them in the process of learning behaviours.

Note: Where the term 'parents' is used in this book, it refers to all those people who might take on the parental role, such as step-parents, foster parents, adoptive parents, family members, and so on.

Sue Cowley

www.suecowley.co.uk

Chapter One

Behaviour is Communication

In this chapter:

  ✓ Think about what we mean when we talk about 'behaviour'.

  ✓ Explore the idea of behaviour as a form of communication.

  ✓ Understand more about what your children's behaviour is communicating.

  ✓ Think about yourself as a role model of effective communication.

  ✓ Look at how, why and what staff behaviour communicates to the children.

Everything we do is essentially behaviour. The word simply describes the acts and actions of human beings – the way we conduct ourselves – particularly in relation to others. However, as well as behaviour being a fact of our existence, in an educational setting we also need to learn how to behave in a way that allows us and others to learn. This is a crucial aspect of the work we do as early years educators – we are building the foundations for our children to have a successful experience within the education system as a whole.

We need to help our children understand what it looks like to behave in an appropriate way – learning to control our behaviours so that we are supportive of the aims of the community as a whole. This community might be a family group, a neighbourhood, an early years setting, a class, a school, a workplace. In order to take our place in that community and to allow the community to function at its best, we need to follow a commonly held set of expectations about how people 'should behave' within it.

Behaviour as a form of communication

When considering how to help children in learning how to behave within our settings and within their wider communities, it is very useful to think of their behaviour – and ours – as a form of communication. In the same way that we would try to assess 'where a child is at' when we aim to support them in developing their learning, so we need to figure out 'where a child is at' when our aim is to support them in developing their behaviour. One of our core roles as early years educators is to help our children with their personal, social and emotional development. When we think about the work we do supporting the 'whole child', this includes all aspects of the children's care, learning and development.

If we see behaviour as a form of communication, and we can learn how to interpret the behaviours we see, we may find out a lot about our children's thoughts, needs, difficulties, experiences, emotions, ideas and ways of learning. This is not the same thing as saying that all behaviours are equally explicable, or that we must pay attention to and interpret every behaviour that we see. However, if we can learn to appreciate the factors that might impact on a child's level of understanding of what 'appropriate behaviour' means, we can help the child build on their current level of skill in 'behaving appropriately'.

Play and positive behaviours

When we talk about 'behaviour' in education, it tends to be with a sigh and a set of worries about the behaviours that are difficult to deal with. However, it is well worth remembering that most behaviours we see in our settings are highly positive behaviours that we actively want the children to develop. When we watch our children's behaviours as they play, we see learning in action. During their play, children develop a wide range of skills, build their physical strength, develop socialisation and resolve conflicts, make friends, explore their world, and boost their physical and emotional skills. Play is a very powerful tool through which children communicate their views of the world. The exploratory and experimental behaviours we see children participate in during play are vital for healthy child development.

Through their play, we see children engaged in lots of really important aspects of early child development, including:

✓ cooperative behaviours.

✓ exploratory and experimental behaviours.

✓ persistence and resilience.

✓ understanding the world around them and how it works.

✓ exploring symbolic and figurative communication.

✓ imagining and creating.

✓ learning to cope with difficulty and challenge.

✓ building focus and attention – achieving the state of 'flow'.

✓ social behaviours – making friends and getting on with others.

What factors impact on young children's behaviour?

There are various factors that are specific to the behaviours that we see in babies, toddlers and young children. It is important to be aware of the range of elements at work here, because this can help us figure out what is going on for the individual child. Once we understand this, we are better placed to meet the child's needs or to help them adapt and deal with what is going on for them. We should bear in mind that:

✓ Young children cannot easily express or communicate their thoughts, emotions and experiences to adults, because they do not yet have the language to do so.

✓ Young children are still developing the ability to understand and control their own impulses and to self-regulate.

✓ Young children look to adults to learn from and to build their repertoire of expected behaviours and ways of approaching tasks.

✓ Young children have not yet learned the expected behaviours within different social situations – they do not yet understand fully what 'appropriate behaviour' looks like.

✓ Young children are more affected by both internal and external stimuli – if they are tired, hungry, stressed, over- or under-stimulated, or simply in need of attention or help, this is all shown through their behaviours.

✓ Young children are not necessarily able to explain to us what they are feeling, particularly when they are caught up in the moment of a 'fight or flight' response.

From a baby's cries when it needs to be fed, to a toddler who throws a toy in frustration, young children send us a series of important messages in their behaviours about what they are thinking and feeling. All these behaviours are perfectly normal, which is why it is unhelpful to label them as 'misbehaviour'. Always bear in mind that this is part of a learning process, not a judgement about the child. Remember too that behaviour can communicate positive as well as negative messages: smiles and laughter communicate the welcome message that children are happy and at ease. We should always aim to look out for these positive behaviours as well as try to understand any problematic ones.

Becoming a 'child whisperer'

Because young children do not yet have the ability to understand or express what is going on for them fully, practitioners and teachers must become highly attuned to many different forms of communication. By learning to interpret the behaviours we see, we can try to figure out what is going on internally for the child and consequently respond to it in the most helpful or appropriate way. If we are open to seeing our children's behaviour as a way for them to express what is going on internally, we can learn a great deal from them, even if they are not yet able to put it into words. We can also support them in learning to communicate their needs and emotions more effectively.

To become a 'child whisperer', educators must learn to:

✓ read children's body language and posture and how these can change over time.

✓ notice and respond to children's facial expressions as an indicator of mood.

✓ become sensitive to how a child is reacting to the practitioner's input.

✓ understand the likely triggers for certain behaviours in a child.

✓ look at how children are interacting with their peers for clues as to what is going on internally.

All these factors can help us pick up on what is being communicated by different behaviours, even without the child being able to explain them in words. Looking for and understanding these signals can help us to distract from or defuse a situation where we see that some problematic behaviour is about to occur. For instance, there are often a number of signals that a child is building up to a tantrum – tense body language, a fixed stare, a scrunched-up face, indicators that the child is tired or hungry. Once you have 'tuned in to' a child, depending on what you 'read' you might respond in a wide range of ways. For instance, you could:

✓ turn towards them.

✓ adopt a relaxed posture.

✓ move in towards them or conversely allow them more space.

✓ repeat what they have said.

✓ nod in agreement.

✓ use a calming tone to bring down their emotional state.

✓ simply smile at them.

A new way of looking

Thinking about behaviour as communication offers us a new way of looking at behaviour, because it lets us stop thinking of the behaviour as being about us and helps us start thinking about it as being about the child. The child whom we might read as 'defiant' on the surface is telling us something about how they feel in the situation in which they find themselves. This is categorically not to say that we must attend to everything that is communicated by inappropriate behaviour, nor that we should somehow excuse it or wave it away. Sometimes, what we see is a behaviour that is best ignored in order to support the child. It is fine for practitioners and teachers to decide not to react at times, just as it is fine to respond to what is being communicated to them.

Seeing behaviour as a form of communication helps you to stop taking it personally when a child misbehaves. It is very rarely the case that young children's behaviour is a calculated attempt to upset adults or to wind them up. They are just not that premeditated; nor do young children have that level of control over their own behaviours. The behaviour we see in our youngest learners is usually about an inability to control their impulses or a reaction to some underlying cause. With young children, often the best first approach is to 'co-regulate' – to acknowledge and accept the behaviour and then to support the child in stopping it or dealing with it.

How do babies and children learn to communicate?

When thinking about behaviour as a form of communication, it is useful to understand how the skill of communication develops. This helps us to see why children might use their behaviour to communicate messages that would probably be more helpfully sent in other ways. In order to communicate effectively, children need to learn and develop a range of key skills – skills that develop over time and that are in their infancy for this age group. In the Early Years Foundation Stage (EYFS) statutory guidance in England, the skill of communication mostly falls under 'Communication and Language', but also forms part of 'Personal, Social and Emotional Development'. There are also elements of communication in 'Expressive Arts and Design' – the arts are very much a form of self-expression.

In order to learn to communicate fully and effectively, young children need to:

✓ form relationships with the adults and peers around them and learn how to interact with them.

✓ play and 'play around with' communication in a variety of different environments, to start to understand how communication works.

✓ be able to pick out sounds in the environment and understand what those sounds mean.

✓ learn to interpret some of the subtleties of verbal communication, such as tone, inference, and so on.

✓ develop spoken language or, where this is not possible, forms of non-verbal communication.

✓ build a wide enough vocabulary to express what they want to say.

✓ understand and make use of non-verbal signals and facial expressions to understand others and to support what they themselves are communicating.

✓ learn to listen and pay attention to a situation, or to what is being said to them.

✓ be motivated and confident enough to interact with others – communication is an act of social engagement.

✓ trust and believe that they will be listened to by the people around them.

As you can see – it's a lot to learn!

For newborn babies, the first acts of communication are instinctive and non-verbal – typically cries and other vocal sounds. Babies obviously do not yet understand what the sounds they hear mean, nor are they able to understand those sounds as individual words. They have not yet developed the facial muscles needed to form words themselves either. When a baby cries, we don't say it is 'misbehaving'. We attend to what it is trying to tell us and we aim to meet its needs. The concept of 'misbehaviour' that often imbues educational discussions is a description of something that doesn't really exist for young children. Their behaviours are instinctive and rarely what we might call deliberate or premeditated.

Interestingly, a baby is born with the ability to learn and speak any language, and it is only the environment in which they find themselves that defines which language they will learn – nurture plays a key role in all aspects of development. When adults are playing and communicating with babies, you will often see them combining speech with gesture – for instance, waving to someone and saying 'bye bye' at the same time – to model what the gesture and the words together mean. Gradually, babies begin to babble to communicate and express themselves, before moving on to form single words, use phrases and finally speak in sentences.

The development of speaking and listening clearly plays a crucial role in young children's learning and development, because this allows them to gather information and communicate more easily with others. It enables them to participate in play with their peers and to articulate their ideas. By learning to talk, children can express their thoughts and learn more about their world. Talk helps to build the skills needed for literacy, allowing children to acquire a wide and varied vocabulary. The development of speech is also crucial for learning behaviours, because it allows children to start expressing what they need to others – whether that is their peers when they are playing with them or the adults who care for and educate them. Over the years, numerous studies have found a link between delays and difficulties in language development and problems with behaviour.

Clearly, we need to be conscious of what all this means for children who have some kind of hearing impairment, or who encounter difficulties with speech and language development. We need to build communication in all its forms in our settings – using signing systems such as Makaton and other visual aids to support children to communicate in a whole range of different ways. We also need to be alert for children whose communication seems delayed, tracking their development carefully and working closely with speech and language therapists as necessary.

Physical communication

Young children will often resort to physical actions to let the adults know how they are feeling. Sometimes these acts are an attempt to soothe pain or discomfort that the child is experiencing; other times they seem to be a reaction triggered by a particular frustration or difficulty faced by the child. Small children have not yet developed impulse control, and they are unlikely to fully understand social expectations around physical communication, so it is not surprising that they might lash out physically when they feel stressed.

Biting is a well-known behaviour in the early years – particularly when young children are teething. Babies will bite on teething rings, toys, perhaps a dummy, or even give a nip to their parents' fingers or shoulders (or worse, if you're a mum who is breastfeeding). It is fairly common for small children to lash out physically in reaction to stressful situations – for instance, if they feel cornered, trapped or under threat. Sometimes the two come together, and a small child will bite another child or an adult. This can be very distressing for all concerned, but it is actually a fairly common occurrence, particularly in the youngest part of this age group. You can find a case study about dealing with children who bite in the last chapter of this book.

Of course, physical communication is not just about negatives. Young children express themselves physically in all kinds of ways – giving hugs, jumping for joy, holding hands with a friend. With rapidly developing bodies and a limited understanding of language, it makes sense that our youngest learners use physical communication a great deal. Again, aim to focus on the positive behaviours, highlighting and responding affirmatively to these, rather than giving all your attention to negative physical communication.

Physical acts of aggression can happen for a range of reasons. It may be that:

✓ the child has not yet learned enough language to express their fears and frustrations, or is not able to reach for the vocabulary that is needed.

✓ they have not yet developed the self-control and self-awareness needed to manage their anger or emotions and so they lash out on impulse.

✓ the child has developmental issues, for instance, the child has experienced some kind of sensory deprivation in the past, or is currently experiencing it.

✓ the physical communication is a sign of a special educational need that needs exploring and identifying.

✓ the child is in pain, and the act of physical aggression soothes that feeling.

How can we support communication?

In the early years, one of the best ways to develop language and understanding is through play, and through adults using what are referred to as 'serve and return conversations'. This means interactions with warm and attentive carers where both child and adult participate in the act of communication. Of course, we don't wait until a child is already speaking to talk with them. We chat to a baby and they respond, at first with facial expressions, though very soon they begin to babble back. Every interaction we have with a child demonstrates to them that speech can be used to communicate, and also that we can communicate by using gestures, facial expressions, and so on. Play is hugely important in the development of communication because it is through play that children learn to interact both with other people and with the world.

Practitioners should always bear in mind that facial expressions, tone and gesture play a crucial role in these serve and return conversations. These aspects help us to communicate meaning before the child understands the vocabulary we are using, and also help the child to understand more about all the different forms of communication. Consider how it feels when you are overseas and trying to make sense of a language that you don't speak fluently – just like when you were a baby, you will gather meaning from the cues and clues that sit around the vocabulary itself. You will also use those same non-verbal gestures and perhaps a few stilted sounds to try to make yourself understood.

For high-quality talk and communication to take place and communication skills to develop, it is important to remember the following:

✓ Children need a rich range of play experiences and enabling environments in order to have something to explore, engage with and communicate about.

✓ Children need to learn how to both speak *and* to listen. Ensure that you offer opportunities for them to tune in to different kinds of sounds during their time in your setting, as well as to make those sounds.

✓ If the noise levels in a setting become too high, they can interfere with the quality of the speaking and listening that takes place. Balance periods of quiet to aid concentration and support children's phonological development.

✓ Quieter times or spaces in your setting help children focus on their learning and on quieter types of play. This will also help them to feel calm and will be very useful if they are feeling tired.

✓ When you are interacting with your children as they play, you should make sure that you listen in order to hear what they are saying, rather than listening just in order to wait your turn to speak.

It is a considerable skill to fully tune in to what children are 'saying' to us, whether this is through their faces, gestures, words, tone or posture.

What is behaviour communicating?

When we view behaviour as a form of communication, we need to find a way to work out what is being communicated. It is fairly easy to observe when a child is happy or enjoying their learning, because you will see them laugh and smile as they play. However, it is a human tendency to jump to conclusions and snap judgements around negative behaviours, especially when it comes to those of other people. We are prone to a series of 'biases' that cause us to do this. For instance, it is tempting to use words such as 'lazy' or 'defiant' when a child or young person behaves in a way that annoys or irritates us – to use words which make a judgement about the reasons for the behaviour. Often, we do this instinctively and without considering whether there could be a different explanation.

When thinking about behaviour as communication, it is useful to view this process as being about removing barriers. If behaviour 'x' is caused by barrier 'y', and doing 'z' would remove 'y' as a barrier, then it supports the child to remove 'y'. We can pre-empt the behaviour by ensuring that the things that trigger the behaviour do not occur. For instance, including a mid-morning snack to ensure that children eat regularly will help you minimise problems around inappropriate behaviours caused by low blood sugar levels. This acts as a way of co-regulating for the child, and consequently feeds into the child being able to develop self-regulation.

Behaviour: biology and physiology

As a first step when exploring what young children's behaviour might be communicating, it is helpful to consider the possibility of a biological or physiological cause. Young children in particular are basically hostages to their biology: until they have developed some impulse control and self-regulation, they naturally react to how their body makes them feel. Behaviour in babies and toddlers has in essence evolved as a survival mechanism; without an adult to care for and feed them, they would not survive. Communicating their needs, through whatever method is available, is critical. A baby's cries alert the adults that they need to help the baby. As we see in many sad cases, neglect of children actually causes damage to early brain development, in addition to the more obvious outward physical signs such as weight loss from malnutrition. This can in turn contribute to problems with impulsive behaviours. Being attuned to babies and young children is crucial for their healthy development.

Additionally, there may be other things going on for a young child that they simply cannot express to their carers – for instance, the crying of a baby or toddler may be a warning that they are in pain because they are teething or have a fever or nappy rash. (It has been said that it is a very good thing that we are not able to remember how painful teething was, because we would be horrified at the level of pain we felt.) Even as we mature and become adults, these biological and physiological causes of poor behaviour still hold us in their sway. Think about how you are much more likely to end up having a row with your partner if you are both over-tired or your blood sugar levels are low.

Adults can usually cope to an extent with feeling hungry, and we are usually aware that if we start to feel lethargic, it might be a good idea for us to have something to eat. We also create routines for ourselves ('elevenses') to counteract the likelihood of the issue occurring. Children do not have the ability to reflect on and react to their physical state in this way – this is one of the reasons why early years settings typically include a 'snack time' between the children arriving in a setting and lunchtime. If you have a late lunchtime in your school or setting, it is useful to analyse patterns of behaviour in the time period before lunch. Consider whether any poor behaviour at this time might simply reflect a dip in energy levels for your children.

Where we can figure out the underlying cause of the behaviour, we can then take this into account as we try to solve the problem. And if our first assumption isn't right, we can then delve more deeply into what is going on in an attempt to figure out what other things may be happening. Look at the case studies in Chapter 9 to think about some of the things that behaviours could be communicating and what we might do to resolve them.

Chapter Two

The Expert Communicator

In this chapter:

- ✓ Understand more about how communication works.

- ✓ Think about how and what children learn from practitioners as role models.

- ✓ Improve behaviour by developing your skill as an expert communicator.

- ✓ Build your skills in verbal and non-verbal communication.

- ✓ Learn more about the role of talk in learning behaviours.

- ✓ Help families achieve better behaviour through effective communication.

While children communicate to us through their play and behaviours, communication flows in the opposite direction as well. Our children pick up and learn from the behaviours that both the adults and their peers model for them when they are together. Where these behaviours are playful, joyful, exploratory and cooperative, the children build a sense of how the world looks when things are working well. For some children, this might simply provide a continuation of how things feel at home, whereas for others it might offer an alternative model from which they can learn about communication and cooperation.

Clearly, the key models of behaviour during early childhood are the parents – babies and young children generally spend much more time with their parents or carers than with anyone else during this period of their lives. Specific patterns of behaviour may have been modelled for the child, sometimes for several years, before they start in our settings. While this is often a positive, because parents have modelled the kind of behaviours that we might refer to as 'appropriate' ones, it can also be a negative, because children may have picked up negative habits that are difficult for us to change.

We tend to think of communication as being mainly about people using language – speaking or writing to each other, for instance. But it is much more than that, because so much of communication is unspoken. We can communicate one message with what we say, while at the same time communicating entirely the opposite message with what we do. A great example of this is the teacher who sets the expectation of silent listening, but who then proceeds to talk over their class. We need to ensure that what we communicate with our words is backed up by what we communicate with our actions, in order to build the best climate for self-regulation to develop.

Being a role model

As practitioners, we need to act as positive role models of all different kinds of behaviours, just as we need to act as positive role models of learning. Practitioners and teachers in the early years must be expert communicators, because this is one of the keys for achieving positive outcomes in your setting. We need to be able to communicate well in order to support the children's learning as they play, and we must also be able to communicate well to aid the children in learning a range of behaviours. Remember that all communications act as a teaching model – both positive and negative – for your children learning to communicate.

Consider for a moment the impact of what we do as adults on the way that children behave when they are with us (and indeed when they are not). Child and adult behaviour are inextricably linked – we are not only educating our children in behaviour, but we are also acting as role models of behaviour. We acknowledge the role of modelling in behaviour every time we express frustration about how parents 'just don't teach their kids to behave any more' or when we link a lack of boundaries in the home with the inappropriate behaviour we see in our settings. Children pick up habits of behaviour over time, and it can be hard for settings to overlay any negative habits with more positive ones.

Right from the moment they are born, children start to react and respond to the people around them. This is one reason why it is so important for them to have responsive caregivers. It is also the reason why you might sometimes experience swearing from a very young child: if a child hears their parents, or those around them, using swear words all the time, they can easily pick these up and then repeat them in a setting. Even though they have no idea of the meaning behind what they are saying, they 'model' the behaviour that they have experienced in the home.

The practitioner as role model

Our first step as educators should always be to model – in all our interactions with the children – the behaviours we expect to receive. This includes taking a positive, engaged attitude as we join in their group play, as well as considering how we interact with individual children about what they are doing. As the paid adults within the relationship, it is our duty to present the best possible model, no matter how difficult that might be when we are faced with difficult to handle behaviours. While our instinct might be to react defensively, in the long run that is not an effective or appropriate response. In order to be an effective role model, it is important for us to reflect on our own behaviours when we do not get things completely right.

Where there are strong relationships, children look to practitioners and teachers as models of what is both possible and desirable. This is why it is so important to have a diverse range of role models for them to see: it shows them the possibilities, and it helps them to understand the way that people can fulfil different roles, including that of caregiver. Remember that the act of role modelling extends beyond practitioners and parents. Members of the wider family (e.g. grandparents) can be powerful role models, as can other people within the local community, such as 'people who help us' (e.g. police officers and medical staff).

In order to be an effective role model:

✓ Think about how you talk, considering the volume of your speech as well as what you say. When adults talk quietly, they encourage the children to listen carefully. It really is worth speaking *more quietly* than the children you work with.

✓ Remember that the children are looking at and listening to you all the time, even when you are not directly addressing them. Your entire approach is part of the 'model' that you present.

✓ Model the behaviour that you want your children to learn through different moments during the day. For example, if you want to help a child understand how to introduce themselves into peer group play, demonstrate some phrases it is helpful to use, modelling these when the child is watching. (For instance: 'Is it okay if I join in with your game?' or 'Can I have a go with that next, please?')

✓ Remember that when you play with or alongside a child, you are modelling various behaviours for them. This includes your attitude to learning (curiosity, interest, focus) and the vocabulary you use.

✓ Constantly model the use of modulation in your speech. Tone is a very powerful tool to aid understanding, and it also triggers the part of the brain that deals with emotions, so it can help support the development of empathy and relationships.

✓ Use sustained shared thinking to help your children understand how to express and build on their ideas. This approach shows children how exploration and curiosity are powerful aspects of learning.

✓ Learn to control your instinctive responses. When we are tired or stressed, our tempers tend to get short and our style of communication can change. If you feel yourself getting irritated, take a moment for a few deep breaths before you respond to a child. Remember that you are modelling what 'self-control' looks like for your children when you react calmly to difficulties.

The way you behave as a teacher or practitioner does not have to be exactly the same as you behave when you are not at work. I like to think of 'putting on' my 'teacher character' when I am working with learners of any age. My character is not quite the same 'me' in day-to-day life; it is a slightly exaggerated version of all the parts of my personality that are most likely to help learning and positive behaviour happen.

Effective non-verbal communication

We tend to think of communication as being about talk, but in fact it is so much more than that. With the youngest age group, where language is not yet fully developed, non-verbal cues are as important (if not more so) than verbal ones. We communicate non-verbally all the time: sometimes deliberately, but often at a subconscious level where we are not even aware of what we are doing. Non-verbal communication can take place in lots of different parts of our bodies. Non-verbal communication can take a range of forms, including:

→ our facial expressions – a frown, a smile, raised eyebrows, wide open eyes.

→ the posture of our bodies – tense, relaxed, upright, defensive.

→ hand gestures – signalling stop, hurry up, well done.

→ the way we move our bodies – a shrug, suddenly going still, trudging tiredly.

To make the most effective use of non-verbal communication, practitioners need to become adept at using their bodies to communicate information to the children. This is very similar to the way in which an actor works on the stage – the audience 'reads' the small cues and clues as well as listening to what is being said. For instance, you might:

✓ raise your eyebrows and open your eyes wide to indicate surprise and pleasure at something a child has done.

✓ smile and wrinkle up your nose to demonstrate how happy you are to see a child.

✓ put a finger to your lips and pause, very still, to indicate that you are waiting for silence.

✓ place your hand on your chin and half-close your eyes to show that you are puzzled at something that is going on.

✓ move slightly towards or away from the child, depending on what you want to communicate.

Remember that practitioners not only need to become effective at using non-verbal communication themselves, but also at reading it in the children. Where you learn to spot the early non-verbal signals that a child is becoming upset or is having a problem of some kind, you can intervene to try to stop the issue building to a head. Young children will often tense up, or their faces will crease up to show stress, when they are feeling anxious or nervous.

Effective verbal communication

We use our voices for many reasons: to talk with the children, to explain the learning, to draw in the children and encourage them to listen, to create a sense of excitement, to calm down a class. Talk is crucial in helping the children to learn and develop, to understand the curriculum, and in supporting them to attain a wide vocabulary as their language develops. Talk also plays a key role in learning behaviour – often young children's behaviour issues are about misunderstandings and frustrations rather than a deliberate attempt to be difficult. The more that they understand what we are saying to them and are able to express themselves to us in return, the less likely they are to encounter difficulties and frustrations around behaviour.

One of the key factors for effective practice in all areas of the early years is to ensure that an extremely high quality of talk goes on in your setting. This will have a powerful impact on how the children's language and communication skills develop, and consequently on how they learn and develop behaviourally. When we consider how best to use our voices, it is important to think about both *what* we say and *how* we say it.

Thinking about what we say

Working with young children means that we have to think very carefully about the vocabulary we use. We need to balance our desire to develop children's vocabulary with the need for what we say to be understood. It can be tempting for adults to adopt a kind of 'baby talk' when they are working with young children, and sometimes this will be appropriate –

for instance, when you are babbling playfully with a baby. However, it is usually best to model normal speech for young children, while at the same time thinking carefully about the particular vocabulary or terminology you use to make what you say to them as accessible as possible.

When we are talking with children, we also need to do the following:

✓ Frame what we say in a positive manner. Think about what we do want from the children in terms of their learning and behaviour, rather than what we don't.

✓ Use inclusive language to create a feeling of cooperation and to boost the children's sense of the setting being a community – aiming to use 'we' and 'us' rather than 'I' and 'you'.

✓ Take care to avoid rhetorical questions. These are typically an expression of frustration ('Why are you doing that?') and can be confusing for children because they will probably take what we say literally.

✓ Consider how clarity of instructions leads to improved behaviour, because it allows the children to understand what we are asking of them.

✓ Minimise the number of instructions we give at any one time, to avoid overloading the children and causing confusion.

Think also about how long you talk to the children for at any one time. Young children have not yet built up their ability to focus. If you try to make them pay attention to what you are saying for longer than they are able to, they are likely to become distracted and stop listening. A useful though very rough rule of thumb for the amount of time that young children can concentrate on an adult talking, without any other interactions being involved, is 'their age plus 2'. This is, of course, a generalisation; some children will be able to concentrate for much longer and some for much shorter a time. Much will also depend on what it is you are asking them to do.

We need to take account of the children's concentration levels when we are addressing the group as a whole. We also need to bear in mind that different children within that group will have different needs, and that they will also be different ages (even within the same year group in a school-based early years setting). We should respond appropriately to the knowledge we have of our children. So, for instance, if you are reading a story, create opportunities for the children to answer in character, or to act out some of what is happening. Once you get past the limits of their concentration, you will tend to see young children wriggling and squirming on the carpet, getting up to drift away, or even falling asleep.

Thinking about how we talk

As 'expert communicators', we need to constantly reflect on the way that we use our voices. Children will typically focus more on the sound of what we are saying than on the content of the words. This is especially so if they don't yet have much vocabulary knowledge themselves and are still in the first stages of learning to speak. Remember that all those cues and clues that you give about meaning through the sound of your voice work even better the more you exaggerate them. You can be especially playful when you are reading stories to the children.

There are various factors involved in the way we talk – these include our tone, volume levels, the pace of our speech and the pitch at which we speak. Below are some thoughts about how you can become more expert in all of these areas.

Thinking about vocal tone:

✓ When you talk to the group as a whole, use lots of tone in your voice to help the children tune in to what you are saying. Young children and those who have English as an additional language find high levels of tone especially useful in understanding what is being said.

✓ Remember that it is almost impossible to overdo the amount of tone you put in your voice, especially with this age group. Aim to sound really surprised, really excited, really curious, and so on. Young children pick up a lot of cues and clues from vocal tone, so it is worth exaggerating what you might do in your normal daily speech outside of the setting.

✓ Always aim to check for understanding, rather than assuming that because it has been said it has been heard and understood. You can do this by a simple process of asking questions to gauge understanding, or by getting some kind of feedback from the group.

Thinking about volume:

✓ Draw in the children by using a quiet voice. Combine this with leaning towards them a little to 'gather them in' for the most powerful effect.

✓ Speak a touch quieter than you might think you need to. This encourages the children to listen and to focus – two key self-regulation skills that they will need to develop in order to get the best out of their educational experiences.

✓ If you catch your voice going too loud – perhaps because you are stressed or because the children are being noisy – take a pause, take a breath, and lower your volume. A sudden drop in volume can be really effective.

Thinking about pace:

✓ Slow down your pace and use lots of repetition to aid understanding. Don't be afraid to say the same thing in several different ways to make sure that the children understand.

✓ Use pauses to gain the attention of the group or the class and to create moments of calm. It can feel tricky to pause and wait, but it is an excellent way of supporting the children in bringing their attention to you.

✓ As well as thinking about the pace of your speech generally, it is also useful to think about the pacing of individual words. For instance, you can put added emphasis on a key word that you want the children to pick up by slowing down as you say it.

Thinking about pitch:

✓ We tend to associate pitch with gender, and to some extent this is correct, because generally speaking women's voices are at a higher pitch than those of men. (This is to do with the length of women's vocal cords in contrast to men's.)

✓ Despite the gender difference, however, it is perfectly possible to adapt your pitch, just as you can adapt the tone or volume of your voice.

✓ Our pitch tends to go up when we are under stress, and a higher pitch can create a feeling of tension in the atmosphere. Aim deliberately to lower your pitch to aid the sense of calm.

✓ You can create a lower pitch in your voice by relaxing your vocal folds. Focus on the base of your neck and deliberately aim to relax the tension in that area of your throat as you speak.

Talking stories

Your daily story times provide a key opportunity for you, as an 'expert communicator', both to model effective communication and to support the children in learning behaviours. High-quality voice usage is really important when you are reading stories to the children – it aids their understanding and helps them to engage and learn. The children will be picking up lots of clues about the stories you read to them through the way you incorporate tone. Adding interest to your voice will also help them focus on the story and will motivate them to listen and in turn develop their phonological awareness.

A lot of behaviours linked to self-regulation can be learned, built and developed during story times. When we read a whole group or whole class story, the children are building their ability to focus, to pay attention, to pick out the sounds of words and the meaning of the story, to (preferably) sit still, to take turns, to share, and so on. Reading stories to a group of children is a bit more difficult and complicated than reading one-to-one with a child. In a mixed age setting, or where there are children with significant additional needs, it can sometimes be hard to engage everyone's focus at the same time. Follow the advice below to get the most out of 'talking stories':

✓ Learn to read upside down, so that you can hold the book towards the children as you read it to them. This way they can see the pictures and you can see each other's faces.

✓ If you find it too tricky to read upside down, then hold the book out to one side to read it instead.

✓ Alternatively, you can use a 'big book' version of books on a stand, if these are available, so that everyone can see the pages and follow the story easily.

✓ Add lots of interest to the story by adapting pitch, volume, tone and pace, speeding up for the exciting bits and slowing down for the quiet ones.

✓ Keep the children involved by giving them lines to say along with you, or by asking questions about what happens next. Give them a good reason to listen to you and to the story.

✓ Ensure that you incorporate chances for interactions – for instance, asking all the children to act out part of the story as you read – jumping up and climbing a tree with a character, or acting as though they are different animal characters.

✓ Use your face to add interest and meaning. Widen your eyes in wonder or raise your eyebrows in surprise. Adapting your facial expressions also helps you remember to add tone to the way you read.

✓ Incorporate funny accents into the dialogue in stories and create different voices for different characters to help the children differentiate between them.

Reflection activity

Work as a staff team to consider your strengths and weaknesses. How and where is good practice modelled in your setting? Talk together about:

✓ how well you maintain an appropriate level of volume during the course of the setting day.

✓ whether you have noticed that the volume goes up during interactions where practitioners or children are stressed.

✓ what practitioners do to vary the volume, tone and pitch in their voices and in what circumstances this happens.

✓ how well staff use different tones to communicate different emotions, for instance, curiosity, surprise, disappointment and excitement.

✓ how confident the practitioners feel about reading stories to groups of children and how creative they are with their voices when sharing books.

✓ what kind of strategies staff use to build the children's vocabulary.

Building vocabulary

It is important for children to develop a rich, broad and wide vocabulary – the more words they have in their spoken vocabulary, the more easily they can think about and express their own ideas and feelings, and the more easily they will be able to think about and consider their behaviours and their learning. The more words they understand, the more able they will be to understand the explanations that you give them around learning behaviours – for instance, why it is important to share and be kind. A wide vocabulary feeds into all aspects of learning and allows children to become more independent too.

There are lots of different ways that you can support your children in building their vocabularies. Currently, there is a push from government bodies such as the Department for Education (DfE) and Ofsted for practitioners to 'pre-load' vocabulary (i.e. going through the definitions of words before the children meet them, for instance, in a story). However, this is not helpful in the youngest age group, because it does not mirror the way language is acquired at this age. The range of vocabulary acquisition among your children could also potentially be very wide, and so you might be introducing words that some children have no chance of understanding, but which others already know. In a setting where there are mixed ages of children, some may just be starting to speak, while others could be fairly fluent in spoken language already.

To help young children develop their vocabulary, it is important to:

✓ Remember that 'serve and return' conversations are the most important aspect of your practice in terms of supporting children's emerging language skills. Really focus on staff understanding what high-quality conversations look and sound like.

✓ Give children access to rich and varied learning experiences, opportunities and resources. Include trips, visitors, the arts and access to the outdoors in your provision. The more words that children encounter in real life and authentic situations, and the more often they encounter them, the better they will understand, retain and use those words.

✓ Use lots of real-life objects and opportunities. The more sensory connections the children have to what is being talked about, the better. Those sensory interactions can really help them embed the vocabulary.

✓ Aim to maintain a sense of continuity, so that children revisit the same language over time and see how words link to others. For instance, talking about the different objects that are kept in your 'cabinet of curiosities'. There might be a range of shells or fossils in your cabinet, each with its own particular set of associated words.

✓ Work as a staff team to consider the kind of vocabulary that might be used in the talk and play that goes on around various resources to support the children. Some settings like to put up associated vocabulary in different areas to prompt staff to widen the language they use with the children.

✓ However, resist the temptation to believe that lots of laminated vocabulary signs means that vocabulary is 'done'. It is far more effective to embed the language through talk between practitioners and children with this age group, since most children will not be able to read the words.

✓ Have a 'word of the week' that you challenge children and parents/carers to use in different contexts. This might be something like a 'colour of the week' that you explore in various ways within your provision, or simply something for the children to look out for when they are in the setting.

✓ You could link this to a 'Makaton sign of the week' that is used in the setting daily and shared with parents to encourage them to reinforce it at home. We share a weekly Makaton sign in our blog for parents to use with their children.

EAL and early communication

Children with English as an additional language (EAL) in your setting will be developing their ability to talk in two (or more) languages simultaneously. There are lots of known benefits to bilingualism and multilingualism, and the idea should be celebrated rather than viewed as a deficit. Ensure that you celebrate all the languages that are spoken by the children and their families in your setting – for instance, by asking parents to come in and read the children some stories in their home languages or by learning some phrases in the different community languages yourself.

Many of the approaches that work well for young children who are developing language and for children who have SEND (special educational needs and disabilities) will generally also work well for children who do not yet speak much English. It is all about thinking how we can best communicate in an inclusive manner. You might:

✓ use visuals and symbols to communicate messages without words, so that lack of language does not get in the way.

✓ have a set of 'survival words' (or cards with images) that you help the children to learn quickly – key words such as hello/goodbye/toilet/drink/food, and so on.

✓ ensure that you use plenty of tone when you are speaking, to help you get meaning across without every word being understood.

✓ make effective use of gestures and facial expressions to back up what you are saying and to help the children understand.

✓ encourage the children to work together – translating for and supporting each other's understanding.

Celebrating communication

Although it is speech that tends to come to mind first when we think about communication, we should definitely celebrate all the different forms of communication that go on in our settings. This helps promote its importance and also opens up the possibilities for children who are non-verbal, who have SEND that impacts on their language skills, who do not yet speak English and who are the very youngest in the setting. Remember, communication allows us to help children in learning behaviours and allows the children to express themselves, so it is a really important piece of the early years toolkit.

It is a great idea for early years settings to use sign language systems such as Makaton to aid communication for children with SEND. There are lots of ways in which you can embed signing and other forms of communication in your provision. For instance, in our setting we:

✓ have a Makaton 'sign of the week' which we use daily with the children.

✓ share our Makaton 'sign of the week' with parents via our blog.

✓ use Makaton when we are singing nursery rhymes.

✓ include signing when practitioners are telling the children stories.

✓ incorporate Makaton signs into carpet time and snack time.

Remember to add plenty of visual back-ups to any verbal prompts. With very young children, symbols are a great way to communicate information in the setting – for instance, about golden rules or how to wash their hands. You can find lots of useful resources for developing speech, language and communication on the 'I Can' charity's website: www.ican.org.uk.

Chapter Three
The Importance of Expectations

In this chapter:

- Learn more about the role of expectations in helping children learn behaviours.

- Explore different ways to help your children understand the rules.

- Consider how to reinforce and revisit your expectations over time.

- Understand more about how and why routines help children in self-regulating.

- Explore the role of routines in helping to establish expectations.

- Learn more about the role of intrinsic and extrinsic motivation.

In any novel situation, it is helpful to know what to expect. Explaining what you want and need from your children – establishing your expectations and creating clear routines – is a crucial part of helping them understand more about your setting and how it runs. Helping the children understand your expectations of their behaviour, and why they need to work within the routines you have developed, is also a crucial first step towards helping them in learning behaviours. They need to know what you are asking them to reach for before they can attempt to reach it. They need to know what boundaries and routines are in place before they can learn to follow them.

The key point to remember about expectations and routines is that they are simply a way of helping your children understand and learn what behaviours are and are not okay in a particular context. This is not about creating children who are compliant and obedient to adults – it is about supporting children to develop their self-regulation skills. Obviously, many expectations will be similar whatever context we find ourselves in – it is always best to be polite, to be kind, to share, and so on. However, there will also be some rules that are specific to an educational setting – for instance, expectations about how to line up for a fire drill and routines for what to do on arrival at the setting.

Creating golden rules

The idea of 'golden rules' is widely used within early years settings. These are a short set of positive expectations that make it clear to the children what the expected behaviours look like. In other words, your golden rules arise out of your shared expectations. Discussions around your golden rules will play an important part in helping your children to learn behaviours. These discussions are also crucial for your staff team – everyone needs to be 'singing from the same hymn sheet' for the expectations to be consistent and consistently applied.

The way you devise your golden rules will depend on the type of setting you are working in. In a school-based setting, where the same group of children might be together all or most of the time, teachers will often choose to devise their golden rules together with the class. However, in a preschool or day-care setting, where children might attend for different sessions and varying amounts of time and might be of different ages, a set of golden rules could be devised by staff before being discussed with the children.

When creating golden rules for your setting:

✓ Keep them short and sweet: aim for between three and five key rules. Any more than this and you run the risk of confusing or overloading the children.

✓ If you are working together with the children to devise your rules, you might start with a discussion and brainstorming session about

44

what the children think the rules need to be, before narrowing them down together with the group.

✓ Make sure you use child friendly, positive language. Use statements of 'do this' rather than 'don't do that'.

✓ Consider how you frame your rules. Many settings use the inclusive 'We...' to indicate that everyone in the setting is working together.

✓ Be literal in the way you phrase your golden rules. Young children tend to take what is said literally, so think about your phrasing from a child's perspective rather than that of an adult.

✓ Whatever you choose to do, you need to create 'buy-in' from the children. This means talking about and referring to your rules, and the reason you have them, on a regular basis.

✓ Create a large, simply designed display that you can refer to, and that is within the sight line of the children. It is useful to have your display located close to a carpet area where the children gather as a group, or at the front of the room if you are in a classroom, so that you can refer to them easily and regularly.

✓ Make the display child friendly. For instance, use colours, pictures, images and symbols. Some settings use children's handprints to make their golden rules display more colourful.

✓ Think about how staff can reinforce the rules by catching the children 'doing the right thing' and discuss this in your team meetings.

✓ Have a clear policy, which is understood and designed by the staff as a team, on what will happen if the children do not manage to follow the golden rules.

✓ Remember that any consequences you have do not need to be punitive – they can simply be about reinforcing and thinking about the rules and why you have them.

Revisiting your expectations

It is important to revisit and reinforce your rules regularly rather than assume that your children will understand and retain them the first time they are explained. This is particularly important in group provision, where the children are not necessarily all in the setting at the same times or on the same days. Some children might only be in your setting for a single session or day a week, while others might be with you all day, every day. By revisiting and reinforcing the golden rules, you ensure that all children are included in the learning, and you are embedding the appropriate behaviours.

There is no need to see your expectations around behaviour as being separate from the daily routine in your setting. You can reinforce your expectations as a natural part of the way your setting runs each day. For instance, you can highlight children who are behaving in line with your golden rules to reinforce them – for example, saying, 'I notice that Amjad is following our golden rule about good sitting.' You can highlight your golden rules during different parts of the day – for instance, talking about how the children demonstrate good sharing at snack time when they pass around a plate of fruit, or talking about how the children are being kind when they help their friends in putting on their boots before going outside.

Carpet sessions are a great time to reinforce and revisit your rules, because sitting on the carpet requires a lot of the expectations that are typically part of the golden rules used by most settings. For instance, during carpet time you might reinforce your expectations around:

- ✓ how the children should sit when they are grouped together.
- ✓ kind behaviours, such as making space for others or having 'kind hands'.
- ✓ how the children are building levels of attention and focus.
- ✓ appropriate levels of noise for different activities.
- ✓ what 'good listening' looks like.
- ✓ sharing well with others – for instance, during show and tell.

Think carefully about the messages you send through the rules you set. At our preschool, we had a long discussion about how we should phrase our rule around noise. We wanted the children to understand that different noise levels are appropriate for different situations, rather than just insisting on 'quiet' or 'silence', which would not apply in all circumstances. However, we didn't want our rule to become overly complicated – it had to apply generally to all situations. The 'golden rule' we eventually alighted on had two parts: 'We use our indoor voices inside'; 'We use our outdoor voices outside.'

Reinforcing your expectations

To reinforce your rules over time, you will need to figure out what you are going to do if the children are not following them. The way you react when the children *aren't* following the rules is just as important as the way you react when they are. It is very easy to slip into the habit of highlighting poor behaviours, and by doing so, accidentally reinforcing them. Always start by reinforcing the behaviours you *do* want to see, but be aware of what you will do if you see behaviours that are not appropriate. Make sure you do the following:

✓ Decide on an agreed set of rules, backed up with visual cues, to clarify the behaviour that you want to see in your setting.

✓ Aim to focus on those children who are behaving as you wish. For instance, during carpet times, direct your energy to those children who sit and wait, with their hands in the air, and choose them to answer questions to highlight the required behaviours.

✓ Avoid giving immediate attention to inappropriate behaviours. Try the distract, defer, defuse technique explained below.

✓ When children are not following one of your golden rules, first reinforce the rule that the child should be following by making clear reference to it. You might say, *'Remember our rule: "We always share and take turns."'*

✓ If you need to intervene to resolve the situation, make a statement about the behaviour you want to see rather than talking about the behaviour that you don't want to see. So you might say, *'I need you to give the toy back right away. Thanks.'*

✓ Try ending what you say with 'thanks'. Not only does this model polite language, it also lets the child know that you are assuming they will do as you have asked – and sometimes it works.

✓ Talk about the behaviour as being the problem rather than the child. So, you might say, *'That behaviour is not nice. We do not snatch toys off other people in our nursery.'*

✓ If a child refuses to do as you have asked, explain the choice they need to make. You can do this by using the 'language of choice'. So you might say, *'You have a choice. I need you to give the toy back to Ellie and then we can all carry on playing. Unfortunately, if you won't give the toy back, then we're not going to be able to continue with this game.'*

✓ Have a clear set of procedures in place to deal with disruptive or aggressive behaviour. Take the child to one side and talk through the behaviour, its impact on others, and why it is not appropriate.

✓ Where children refuse point blank to do as you have asked, guide them away from the situation and take them somewhere quiet to have a chat. For instance, in our setting we have a 'thinking spot' (a round rug) where the child and practitioner can go to talk about a problem.

In our setting, we use a 'golden rules song' to reinforce our golden rules. We sing this at carpet time and when the children are getting ready to have their snack. The song is sung to the tune of 'London's Burning' and goes as follows:

'Golden rules, golden rules

Make us happy, keep us safe

Golden rules, golden rules

Don't forget them, or you'll be sad

Golden rules, golden rules.'

You might like to play around with the tunes of some popular nursery rhymes to create your own version of a golden rules song.

Narrating the 'why'

The point about expectations and boundaries is that they form the glue of society – the behaviours we learn support us to become part of our communities and to live and work together in a way that is safe and supportive. We need to help our children understand this by explaining rules and expectations, as well as simply having a set of rules in the first place. Being polite, showing empathy, sharing, thinking of others, doing the right thing – all these behaviours ensure that we can get on with each other and create a kind and inclusive society. When the children know the *why* behind the behaviours that are being asked of them, they are far more likely to cooperate with those expectations. Helping children to learn about the logic behind the behaviours that adults ask for is a really important step in learning behaviours and building good habits.

When you introduce expectations of behaviour, it is really important to narrate the *why* behind the expectations that you have – to talk with the children about why it is important to do these things. A good way to do this is to try to include as often as you can a 'because' when you are talking about behaviours and expectations. So you might say something like:

- ✓ 'We need to keep our hands to ourselves on the carpet ... because other people might not want us to touch them.'

- ✓ 'We need to listen carefully to others ... because that way we can hear what they are saying/take their ideas and opinions into account/learn from them.'

As you talk about your golden rules as a staff team, really think about the 'why' that is going on behind the behaviours you are expecting. By asking staff to make explicit the motivations behind the behaviours, you ensure buy-in from everyone. You also ensure that you don't end up with rules that don't really make sense or that prioritise the needs of adults over the needs of children. If you cannot come up with a 'why' for the rule, it is probably not worth having the rule in the first place. Logically, your rules have to make sense if you are to be able to narrate the 'why' for the children. Where you are working with a whole class in a school-based setting and you have asked the children to develop their golden rules in conjunction with you, again ask them for the 'why' behind the rules they suggest. What is this rule going to help us achieve?

Distract, defer, defuse

Although we quite often need to challenge and talk about inappropriate behaviours in order to help the children to learn different and more appropriate behaviours, it is also the case that quite a lot of low-level behaviour would be more usefully ignored. Having high expectations does not mean always directing your attention towards any child who is not following them. Sometimes, highlighting the behaviour (especially if it is in front of a group) has the effect of not only placing more focus on it, but encouraging the child to repeat the behaviour because they have understood that it is a way to gain attention. It can also result in a child having a meltdown, which is neither useful nor necessary.

The trio of 'distract, defer, defuse' can be really useful to help you remember not to overplay or overreact to inappropriate behaviours.

In order to distract, you might do the following:

- ✓ Ask the child to quickly help you with something: 'Amie, could you come and help me get the snacks ready, thanks?'

- ✓ Point to something to move the child's focus away from the moment: 'Ooh, TJ, look at that bird! What's it doing?'

- ✓ Quickly suggest an alternative activity: 'Why don't we all go and draw a road for the ride-on toys?'

In order to defer, you can do the following:

- ✓ Say to the child that you will talk about something later: 'Let's have a chat about this in a minute, Ahmed, but first why don't we all tidy up the toys?'

- ✓ Get the group started on something else before you have the chat: 'Can you all go and help Lynne with getting the snacks ready while I have a quick word with Charlie? Thanks.'

- ✓ Explain that you will come back in a few minutes to see whether the situation has been resolved: 'I'm going to go and have a look at Millie's tower, but I'll be back in a moment to see whether you've sorted this out between the three of you.'

In order to defuse you can do the following:

✓ Focus on the child, highlighting what you notice about their emotional state: 'I can see that you're really upset about this, Simeon.'

✓ Suggest that the child uses a measure to calm themselves and help them to co-regulate: 'Why don't we take some deep breaths together, Carly?'

Remember to use the children's names as often as you possibly can when you are having these interactions, as this will help to ensure that you have their attention and focus.

The role of routines

Most of us live our lives via a series of routines – we get up at the same time each day to go to work, we put the bins out on a set day each week to catch the refuse collectors, we have our dinner at much the same time each night. Routines help us create a sense of pattern and regularity in our lives – we know what will happen when, and what to expect at different times of the day or week. Routines are also crucial for supporting behaviour and building self-regulation – they form part of your expectations, because they outline expected behaviours at different times of the day. Routines form part of the way that we help the children develop self-regulation, because they ask the children to take responsibility for controlling their own behaviours within the community's framework of requirements. In effect, your setting's routines are a form of co-regulation, where you help the children to regulate their own behaviours.

A key element of an effective early years setting is a sense of routine and a sense of order. This helps the children get into the right place for learning behaviours because it creates a feeling of calm and security. With a clear set of structures in place, the children feel safe to play and learn and they are secure in the knowledge of what is going to happen throughout the day. This is particularly helpful and supportive for any children who have SEND. For children who come from a difficult or chaotic home environment, it may be hard at first to adapt to the expectations of an early years setting. Some children might not understand the thinking behind the structures we have in place – they may never have experienced an environment with clear routines and boundaries before. It is crucial for their success that we help them understand why it is important to play safely and behave sensibly.

Routines give children a feeling of security – they know what is going to happen while they are with us, and when during the day it will happen. Routines help ensure the children's safety and allow us to manage unnecessary risk, because they teach the children how to 'do the right thing' and they introduce a clear element of control and order. Interestingly, routines also support the adults who work in and use the setting – they give staff a set of principles and approaches to use as a team of colleagues. Routines help parents understand what is going to happen during the setting day and to feel secure about leaving their child in our care. Routines help give parents answers to any questions they might have and in turn give them reassurance as well. A clear set of routines will help families understand:

✓ what they should do when they drop off their child at the start of the day.

✓ what their children will be doing and learning at different points during the day.

✓ how the adults are going to manage the group dynamics.

✓ how the adults are going to ensure that the children feel secure.

✓ how the learning will proceed.

✓ what will happen when they pick up their child at the end of the day.

Developing routines for your setting

It is important to work as a staff team to develop a clear set of routines for your setting. We need buy-in from all members of staff to make routines work, because everyone needs to be 'on the same page' about routines and understand them in the same way. We also need everyone's input, because that way staff can highlight any potential issues and make suggestions as to what will work best. Remember that routines do not need to be a 'one time only' decision. They can and should develop and adapt according to the needs of the children who are in the setting at any particular time. In the same way that you regularly revisit and adapt your policies to reflect what happens in practice in your setting, so you should regularly revisit and tweak your routines.

Reflection activity

Work as a staff team to develop a clear set of routines that will really work for your team. Talk together about:

- ✓ what staff feel generally about routines, and the level of structure and control that they feel the children need.

- ✓ how best you can all manage the children's arrival in the mornings, to ensure that they can be as independent as possible.

- ✓ where staff might position themselves in the setting during different parts of the daily routine.

- ✓ how routines can support free flow and help the children become independent in self-care.

- ✓ how parents feel about the setting's routines and any feedback that they have given to staff on this.

- ✓ how children feel about the setting's routines and what opportunities there are for them to contribute to the smooth running of your routines.

When creating routines, there is a balance between controlling the children and helping them learn to behave independently and regulate their behaviour. It is possible to make the setting *too* regulated, controlled and controlling, leaving little space for the children to have autonomy. The routines we create should be purposeful – they need to be there for a specific reason. For each routine you introduce, consider:

- ✓ what the purpose is – e.g. learning, safety, independence, building social skills.

- ✓ how far the children can do this aspect for themselves and how much adult support they will need.

✓ how you will encourage the children to take ownership of the routine.

✓ how you are going to communicate your routines to your children and families and encourage everyone to follow them.

✓ what strategies you can use to achieve staff buy-in to all parts of the routine.

Making the most of routines

The routines that you develop will vary according to the way your day runs, the needs of your children and staff, and the environment within which you work. You will also need to consider how the routines sit alongside the nature of your setting. For instance, routines in a sessional preschool will probably be very different from those in a maintained nursery school or childminder setting. The session and attendance patterns of the children, and the type of setting and building you work from, will have a significant impact on what things like 'drop-off' and 'pick-up' times can look like.

Consider the following points to make the most of routines:

✓ Think about the layout of the space, and how this helps you to direct children and parents to where you need them to go. Consider the flow of the space and how you can avoid any one area becoming overcrowded.

✓ Have visual indicators of routines. If you want the children to put their toy in the show and tell box, put the box somewhere obvious and in their sight lines when they arrive, with a large sign on it.

✓ Use images to help you direct the children's behaviour. Get each child to choose a matching symbol to put on their drawer, coat peg and name tag (e.g. a banana for Bryan).

✓ Think about how you will meet the needs of any children who have SEND or EAL. Will they need extra adult support during the morning routine? What form will this extra support take?

✓ Consider what jobs you want the parents and carers to do, for instance, helping change library books. Encourage parents to support their children in doing these tasks, but not to do all the work for the child. Create WOW goals for the children, e.g. 'WOW: I changed my book by myself!'

✓ Think about where staff are positioned and identify roles and responsibilities for each person. Is one practitioner going to register children and speak to parents while another helps the children settle on the carpet?

It is crucial to think about arrival routines at our settings from the children's perspective as well. This is particularly important in helping us ease transitions into the setting for the children. We need to stand 'in their shoes' and aim to understand their perspective on what our settings look and feel like.

Ask yourself:

✓ How would it feel to be a child in this situation?

✓ Does the atmosphere feel safe, controlled and contained?

✓ Would you know what you are meant to do when you arrive?

✓ How would it feel to be a new starter in this kind of environment?

✓ How might a child who has SEND or EAL feel about being at the setting?

Embedding, clarifying and adapting routines

When you introduce new routines, or adapt existing ones, be sure that everyone understands what the routines are, and why you have them in place – that they have clear expectations and 'narrate the why'. Be clear about the impact of your routines and the benefits of everyone following them. Similarly, be clear about what might happen where the routines are not followed, and why this is problematic. The more open and honest you can be as a staff team about the reasons and motivations behind your structures, the more likely everyone is to work well within them.

Remember too that it is possible for every rule to have an exception – aim for positive reinforcement of your routines rather than a 'do this or else' approach. If an aspect of your routine is proving problematic for lots of families, this might be a 'red flag' that suggests the routine itself is problematic. It is definitely worth revisiting the part of the routine where this happens, to consider where the problem is coming from and how you might adapt the structure to resolve it.

For instance, if you need to ensure a prompt drop-off because you have lots of parents arriving late and the start of the day is being disrupted, it can be tempting just to introduce some kind of punitive measure for lateness. However, you may find it more useful to explore some of the following possibilities:

✓ Be clear both about the required timings and also the *purpose* of having this routine in place.

✓ Explain to parents the positive impact of being on time, for their children and for the setting community as a whole.

✓ Explain how it impacts on the smooth running of the day if children arrive late, for instance, taking staff time away from the children when you are doing carpet time or distracting those who are already settled.

✓ Make it clear that families need to work together for the good of the children and of the setting rather than it being a demand that is being made without any clear purpose.

✓ Be clear that you fully understand that some families will encounter circumstances that are beyond their control and that mean they can't arrive on time.

✓ If it is feasible, consider whether it might be worth adapting your timing to better suit your families.

For instance, in our setting we extended the day by 15 minutes to better fit in with school finishing times, and this had the effect of cutting down on the number of late pick-ups.

You can communicate information about your routines and structures through discussions, or via a blog, a newsletter or an email. Regular reminders are very helpful, while taking care that they don't start to come across as though you are nagging, because this is counterproductive. To embed and clarify routines, it is also useful to do the following:

✓ Create a timetable for staff, showing what the daily routine looks like, so that everyone has a clear idea of what will be happening at different times of day. Chat through this regularly at staff meetings, and make adaptations as required. You could also share this timetable with parents.

✓ Build an understanding of any structures slowly, introducing them gradually, a few at a time. Where you are introducing new routines, consider focusing on one change per week to fully embed it before making any more alterations.

✓ Consider how you might need to adapt the routine for specific children, for instance, those who have SEND or for children of different ages in your setting. A good example of this is carpet time. Some children really struggle with this aspect of provision. In this case, a staff member might lead the child off to a quiet place if they start to be discomforted, or sit beside the child on the carpet during story time to encourage them to stay focused.

Intrinsic and extrinsic motivation

One of the things that practitioners will often ask is how they can motivate their children to follow their expectations. It is important to consider the difference between intrinsic and extrinsic motivators, and how these might impact on children's self-regulation and learning. Young children are naturally motivated to play and to learn through play. From the moment they are born, they are biologically primed to make sense of their world, to process information about it, to interact with it, and to be curious about what is going on around them. This is a key part of how they develop. When you watch a young child exploring their environment, you see this impulse at work: the drive to find out more, through playful exploration, is a hugely powerful motivator.

While we need to have clear expectations of behaviour and sets of rules and routines, it is also crucial for us to help children build on their intrinsic desire to learn. There are, of course, many different factors that can motivate human beings. Some of these are extrinsic (external) and others are intrinsic (internal). Think for a moment about why you turn up to work. To an extent, it is about earning money so that you can pay your rent or keep up repayments on your mortgage. But to an equal and perhaps greater extent, it will be about a whole other set of motivations. If you work in the early years, you are unlikely to be in the job 'just for the money'. There are probably a number of other careers you could have chosen in which you would have earned more.

An interesting observation that has been noted in research into motivation is that extrinsic rewards can actually damage a child's motivation (see John Hattie's work on 'visible learning' and Carol Dweck's work on 'growth mindset' for more on this).[1] It may sound counter-intuitive, but the idea that we would learn or do something 'just for a reward' can be perceived by children as sending the message that we would not do the thing we are doing *unless the reward were there to receive once we'd done it*. Rather than pure behaviourist approaches, thinking in the early years has moved towards the idea that we should aim to encourage intrinsic motivation by avoiding the overuse of extrinsic rewards.

This does not mean that you can never use rewards if you want to, but that the excessive use of rewards is not helpful. For some children, extrinsic rewards can act as a useful 'symbol' that things are going well. However, to maximise intrinsic motivation, you need to make sure that extrinsic rewards do not play too central a role in your practice. The 'reward' of attention, or of your time, can be just as powerful, if not more so, than a sticker or a certificate.

When it comes to using rewards:

- ✓ Catch the children being good. For children who find this challenging, keep a close eye out for examples of them behaving well so that you can highlight them.

- ✓ Consider using rewards that link behaviour in your setting to positive behaviours in the home. For instance, ask parents to fill out a WOW slip.

- ✓ Aim to highlight the behaviour rather than the child. Use language that praises the change in behaviour and focuses on the child's agency ('You're getting so much better at doing that') rather than language that praises the child but suggests that the behaviour is innate ('You're such a clever boy!').

✓ Remember that some children, including those who have SEND, might need some form of extrinsic markers as a symbol of the efforts they are making.

✓ It can work well to have a personalised reward in place for children who really struggle with learning behaviours, as a symbol or marker to indicate that you've noticed their efforts. For instance, you might add a 'WOW' message to the child's learning journey.

In our setting, we made a conscious decision a number of years ago not to use any extrinsic rewards such as stickers, certificates or charts. Our decision was based on the idea that we wanted the learning to be its own reward. Interestingly, our parents and children do not notice the lack of extrinsic rewards.

Chapter Four
From Co-Regulation to Self-Regulation

In this chapter:

✓ Understand more about what 'self-regulation' is and how it develops.

✓ Learn how to put behaviour in the hands of your children.

✓ Explore how staff can help children move from co-regulation to self-regulation.

✓ Appreciate the factors that get in the way of children learning to self-regulate.

✓ Explore the importance of risk-taking and opportunities to fail.

✓ Understand how to support children in becoming independent learners.

Self-regulation has been talked about widely in education in recent years, and for very good reason. Research has shown that there is a clear link between the ability to self-regulate and positive outcomes for children, both while they are in education and in their lives after they leave school. The more that we can help children develop self-regulation in the early years, the better they are likely to do once they start school. Although early years is an important phase in its own right, and should not be seen as a preparation for school, it is vital that we help our children prepare for the transition. One of the key ways in which we can do this is to help them learn to be as independent and self-regulated as possible. Some of the demands that are made of young children in school – to sit still and to listen and focus for increasing periods of time, for example – require a surprisingly high level of skill in this area.

Ideally, the goal for all children as they grow up is to gradually become more independent and to be able to do more and more without adult help. This applies both to their learning and to their behaviours – we want the children to become lifelong learners and to learn to behave in the right way because it is the right thing to do rather than because of some external system that pushes them to behave. To give an example that everyone will recognise, it's important for people to drive at the speed limit even when there is not a traffic officer watching them. Where rules are vital for people's safety, it is problematic if we only stick to them when we think we are going to get caught. The process of building self-regulation starts right from a child's earliest days, and is perhaps nowhere more important than in the early years. If we can set our children up as independent and self-regulated learners right from the word go, this will benefit them in every aspect of their lives.

What is self-regulation?

The term 'self-regulation' describes the ability to have conscious control over our behaviours and actions in response to the situations in which we find ourselves, the stimuli we encounter, or what others need us to do. The term describes a set of cognitive processes that allow us to control our behaviours. These are the mental processes that allow us to plan, focus our attention, manage multiple tasks, and so on. Self-regulation and executive function skills rely on three types of brain function: working memory, mental flexibility and self-control. The term 'executive function' describes the group of skills within our brains that allow us to regulate our own behaviours.[2]

Children are born with the potential to develop these skills, and as practitioners working in the early years, a key part of our work is to help our children develop them. Some children will need more help than others. These are often the children who have encountered some type of adverse experiences during their early years. Self-regulation skills will feed into every aspect of a child's education, allowing them, for instance, to direct their attention to a teacher, or to control the impulse to call out in class. Self-regulation has been found to be highly predictive of future success – in other words, those children who are best able to self-regulate when young tend to have not only the best academic outcomes, but also the best social and emotional outcomes.

The term 'self-regulation' covers the development of various aspects of learning and behaviour, including:

✓ impulse control.

✓ managing our emotional state.

✓ understanding how our behaviours make others feel.

✓ planning how we will learn.

✓ setting ourselves goals.

✓ undertaking and completing challenges.

✓ deciding where to focus our attention.

✓ shifting our attention from one thing to another.

✓ ignoring distractions.

✓ staying focused for increasing periods of time.

✓ recalling information.

✓ understanding how to solve the problems we encounter.

✓ being persistent.

✓ deferring and delaying gratification.

Just as the term 'metacognition' means being aware of and thinking about our own thinking and learning, so self-regulation means helping children to become more aware of their own behaviours, the factors that might impact on those behaviours, and how to control them. We want to encourage children to be able to make better and more conscious decisions about what they will and will not do in different situations. Self-regulation is about building the impulse control that allows us to behave rationally rather than being led by the instinctive responses that are embedded into us through the 'fight or flight' response. Metacognition and self-regulation are closely linked, with a clear relationship between the ability to think about and plan for our own learning (whether academically or behaviourally) as a distinct feature of both terms.

Remember, self-regulation is about far more than just being compliant or following the rules because you are worried about what might happen to you if you break them. For children to learn to fully self-regulate, they need to learn how to do the right things for the right reasons – i.e. whether or not someone is watching and will reward or punish them for what they do. This means that simply having systems that are based on behaviourist principles of rewarding/punishing behaviours is not an effective way to support the development of self-regulation in young children. These systems can send them mixed messages about why they need to learn to behave, and they put the emphasis on external rather than internal controls.

What factors support self-regulation?

The research shows that self-regulation needs some specific conditions to fully develop in young children. The key factors will probably be unsurprising to early years educators – that it is about relationships and challenges – because we see the powerful impact that the home environment can have on children's wellbeing and attainment. The key factors that support self-regulation have been identified as:

- ✓ warm, responsive relationships with trusted and consistent caregivers.
- ✓ an environment that offers sufficient intellectual and physical challenge.
- ✓ classroom practices and processes that offer the child a sense of autonomy.
- ✓ close links to the development of metacognition.

Warm and responsive relationships with caregivers offer children a 'safe space' within which to learn and make mistakes. When they know they will not be judged poorly or found wanting if they make an error, they are far more likely to take the calculated risks that result in intellectual challenge. All educators know the benefits of a positive home environment – of interesting and engaging toys to play with, of relationships with responsive adults – and of being taken outside the home environment to learn new things. Children who are presented with regular challenges in lots of different forms will learn how to plan and manage their approaches and to become persistent in facing them.

Pedagogical approaches that emphasise the child as an active agent, in control of their own selves and their own lives, will help with the development of self-regulation. Where children feel they have autonomy over their learning, at least to some extent, this helps them to build the sense of control that is required to self-regulate. Clearly, this all links very closely to the development of metacognition, because the child is thinking about and controlling their behaviours, which in turn helps them to think about and control their learning.

Deferred gratification

The ability to defer gratification is a central concept within the wider development of self-regulation. The ability to delay or defer gratification is really important for success in education. Delayed gratification basically means the ability to understand and accept that your immediate wishes or desires cannot necessarily be met the moment you have them (if at all), and to have the ability to control those urges until later on. In other words, it is impulse control.

There are a number of reasons why this concept is so important in education. The first is that it is not possible or even desirable for children to receive immediate gratification all the time. This would prevent them from learning self-control and understanding how to work as part of a community. But it is also vital because, as children get older, they will find that it is harder for the teacher to respond to each individual's desires at any one moment. In a class of thirty children, one individual cannot always be the person giving the answer to the teacher's question or being chosen as a volunteer. Similarly, for children to achieve really long-term goals (becoming a vet, for instance), they need to be able to demonstrate persistence over time in reaching that goal. Even if the learning they need to do sometimes feels very hard or dull, the child is able to keep at it in order to achieve the long-term target.

The 'marshmallow experiment', conducted at Stanford University in the 1960s, offers a great insight into how some children are more easily able to regulate their own behaviours, and why it is important for us to help others to learn how to do this. In the experiment, some young children went into a room with a researcher and were offered one marshmallow, which they could eat immediately if they wanted to. However, the researcher also told them that they would come back in twenty minutes, and if the marshmallow was still there, they would receive a second one. You can see some fascinating footage of children taking part in this kind of experiment online.

The researchers tracked what happened to the children, and those who were able to wait for the second marshmallow at a young age had significantly better academic and social outcomes than those who could not. The ability to defer gratification appears to be a strong predictor of positive outcomes later on. In addition, trust seems to play a very important role in deferred gratification. Where children trust that they will receive a greater reward later on if they rely on the adult and bring themselves to wait, this appears to help them to regulate their behaviours. Again, the role of the trusted adult is crucial in helping children persist and consequently in building self-regulation.

What mediates self-regulation?

There is plenty of evidence to suggest that self-regulation is mediated by home background, and by culture/society. In other words, the way in which we are brought up, the resources that we have access to in that environment, and the culture we are brought up in will impact on our ability to think about, adapt to and control our impulses. This will probably be unsurprising to most educators. We see children who have had very little in the way of boundaries put in place at home, or who have experienced difficulties in their early home lives, struggling to self-regulate. We also see the impact of children who have been over-helped: where parents have over-supported a child rather than encouraging them to act independently, the child may struggle to cope if they don't get what they want as soon as they want it.

A recent repeat of the 'marshmallow experiment' found that it was important for the children to perceive the adults as reliable in order for them to be able to wait. If they were in an environment where they were unsure that the adults were reliable, or where they felt they might have to compete for limited resources, they were much more likely to immediately eat the first marshmallow and not wait for the second. This highlights the importance and power of stable and positive relationships and attachments both within the setting and at home. It also demonstrates why it is much harder for some children to self-regulate than it is for others.

Moving from co-regulation to self-regulation

Children and young people do not move straight to self-regulation. They first need the help and support of adults during a process known as co-regulation. The adult gently encourages and supports the children to build control over their own impulses. This is essentially a form of scaffolding – just as we might use a scaffold in the curriculum to support a child to learn something difficult, so we can use a scaffold to help the child in learning behaviours. The adult works alongside the child to support them in becoming more regulated in a variety of situations.

Many of the approaches that you use in your setting will be a form of co-regulation. For instance, the creation of a set of routines is an example of a scaffold within which the children can work. The use of golden rules enables the children to understand the behaviours you are aiming for, and also to think about how the whole learning community needs to work together to achieve these. There are also lots of things that individual practitioners do in their interactions with children that form a key part of co-regulation.

For instance, it could be that the adult:

✓ gently coaxes the child to face a challenge, saying, 'Come on, you can do it' as the child attempts to climb an obstacle.

✓ physically supports the child by offering gentle assistance with an activity or by helping the child to finish a difficult task such as completing a jigsaw.

✓ helps the child to understand their emotional state – for instance, identifying the emotion for the child: 'I can see that you're feeling upset about this.'

✓ supports the child in using self-calming techniques to handle their emotions when they are feeling upset: 'Let's take some deep breaths together.'

✓ models and explains how the child might approach the learning, or works and plays alongside the child as they get to grips with it.

✓ watches from a distance, judging when to step in to offer positive reinforcement and when it is better to stay back.

✓ gently eases the child's way into peer group socialisation – for instance, by joining in with group play alongside the child to help them interact.

✓ strokes the child's back or hugs and soothes the child in order to help them calm down from a tantrum.

Learning to fail

An interesting feature of the development of behaviour is the way that we need to let children genuinely fail and make mistakes in order to help them develop independence and self-regulation. It is not helpful for us to overprotect them and create a buffer against all kinds of failure. As painful as it is for us to watch children fail, we need to sometimes let them make mistakes in order to learn. Of course, this does not mean putting children in line for unacceptable risks or asking children who might struggle to deal with failure to cope without any support. It simply means managing the level of challenge so that the children are stretched, but not beyond their capabilities. You might have heard this idea being referred to as the 'zone of proximal development' – a term that comes from Vygotsky's work on child development.[3] Children need just the right amount of challenge – not too much, not too little – to gradually develop self-regulation and independence.

One of the biggest barriers to our children learning to self-regulate and become independent and trustworthy is a fear of failure. Interestingly, it is often as much about the adult's inability to cope with the child failing as it is about the child being unable to cope with failures of their own. Children only really begin to perceive failure as problematic when they see how adults and other children react to it. The clue is in the term *self-*regulation: we cannot do it for the children; the children must learn to do these things for themselves. Although adults can support children and help them develop their ability to regulate, eventually it has to come from the child. Otherwise, what you are looking at is an external rather than an internal locus of control.

Supporting children to fail

Helping children to build self-regulation by challenging them is not about throwing children in at the deep end without any support. Some children who have not had secure attachments in their earliest years will really struggle to cope when they do not get something right. Other children will present as 'perfectionists' and find the process of making errors very difficult, because it does not fit with their view of themselves and their world. Practitioners need to make careful and sensitive decisions about which children can be stretched at which moments, what challenges are suitable for different children, and how far each child can be stretched.

Co-regulation is crucial in getting children to the point at which they can easily cope with not doing well at something. Some children (typically those with secure attachments) will find it much easier to cope with failure than others, because they have a strong sense of themselves and their place in the world. They trust that loved adults will help and support them if things go wrong, and so any failure does not feel like the end of the world for them. We can help children build their sense of self, and of their rightful place in the world, by giving sensitive feedback that focuses on the child's levels of control rather than on their attainment. For instance, you might say to a child that you were really impressed at how they stuck at it when they were climbing the muddy bank rather than simply praising the child for getting to the top.

Fear of failure

As educators, we will sometimes steer clear of academic situations where children fail, for fear that we won't be able to meet the demands of the curriculum and particularly of statutory tests. We are drawn to over-help and over-support because we have to 'get them through' the work or the test. Thankfully, this is not such a problem in early years, simply because most of the statutory testing (apart from the Foundation Stage Profile in the EYFS) happens when the children are older.

Similarly, we might be worried about how the children will cope with failure. We may feel very reluctant about them being faced with the emotional consequences of the challenges we give them. We can also tend to avoid situations where we allow the children to make mistakes in their behaviours, sometimes for fear of 'what other people will think' if they see us allowing those mistakes to happen. We might worry that other people will think we are simply letting the children get out of control rather than encouraging them to find their own ways to self-regulate.

In many ways, this barrier has been erected by the adults rather than by the child, mainly as a result of the way that our education system itself is run. In a system where accountability consists of high-stakes testing, the temptation is to over-help so that the children do as well as possible. You might have heard of 'helicopter parenting', where the parent hovers over the child, making all the decisions for them and taking them to a series of after-school clubs. In the same way, we can be prone to doing this when we are tempted to over-support the children.

For practitioners, it might often feel like it would be quicker to do things for the children rather than wait for them to go step by step through a process by themselves. It is quicker to help the child put on their shoes than to wait for them to do it (and potentially to do it wrong and have to redo it). For this reason, if we are stressed or in a rush, we might tend to intervene. But every time we step in, over-supporting the child, the child misses out on an opportunity to build independence. Like any skill, independence needs to be learned, and the best way to learn it is through giving it a try, even if that means getting it wrong at first. We need to:

✓ allow children the time and space to take risks and to fail in their learning.

✓ let children make mistakes and then pick up after themselves, rather than swooping in to solve things for them immediately.

✓ pitch the level of challenge high enough so that children are stretched but not over-challenged.

✓ not always correct errors when we spot them – let the children do as much of the work of figuring out how to repair their own mistakes as possible.

✓ put the role of correcting mistakes in the children's hands.

Rather than helping children correct an error when you spot one, simply saying to the child that there is a mistake but that you are confident they will be able to solve it for themselves is a great strategy to support them in repairing their own mistakes. Fear of failure can sometimes tie in to a lack of challenge, because of the concern that we might 'pitch it too high'. Adults can feel nervous about letting children face challenges because of their own fears about what the consequences might be. For instance, the adult might constantly tell the children to 'be careful' when they are playing in a playground. The fear of what might happen if the child falls over can lead us to be over-cautious about the levels of challenge we offer. It is a tricky balance.

Who does the work?

One of the key times at which we need children to regulate their behaviour is when we want the attention of the whole group. This might be because we are going to have a group discussion, do some show and tell, or share a story together. What will sometimes happen at these moments is that the practitioner or teacher will call for the children to be quiet, doing lots of work to get them to settle down. But a better alternative where you are looking to develop self-regulation is to put the behaviour in the hands of the children. In our setting, when it's time to come to the carpet, one of the children rings a bell to signal this. The practitioner sits and waits on a chair at the carpet, giving positive reinforcement to the children as they come to join her, and using non-verbal signals to encourage the children to fall quiet as the group gathers.

Every time the teacher or practitioner works hard to get the children's attention, *they* are doing more of the job of regulation themselves rather than encouraging *the children* to do it for themselves. The pressure of time can make it very hard to fight the urge to 'shush' the children or call for their attention. But in the long run, the ultimate aim needs to be for children to understand the routine – now is the time when we come together and listen to each other – and also why they should fall silent and pay attention – so that the sharing can start.

There are a range of ways to get the children to 'come to you' without actually calling for their attention. You can be as creative with this as you like, and the children will appreciate it if you are imaginative; children love it when adults are playful with this. Most of the time it is useful to agree the signal with the children ahead of time (as in our bell), but sometimes you can also give them a surprise to see how they respond. To get the children to give their attention to you, you might do the following:

✓ Simply pause and wait in your seat, relaxed and patient. This also gives you the chance for a little rest.

✓ Add non-verbal signals to your pause. For instance, raising your eyes to the ceiling or making your body go very still will both indicate 'I'm waiting.'

✓ If you wear a watch, look at this to send the signal about time being precious.

✓ Start talking to the first children who arrive on the carpet, saying how good it is to see them responding so quickly, and thanking them for doing so.

✓ Clap your hands in a pattern, encouraging the children to clap the pattern back to you.

✓ Call out a phrase and get the children to respond to it. This 'call and respond' approach requires you to agree the phrase/response with the children ahead of time. Some teachers use 'One-two-three; eyes on me' with the children responding 'One, two; eyes on you'.

✓ Add sets of gestures or hand signals to your call and respond phrases, to make them even more effective. For instance, the children can count 'one, two' on their fingers, then point to their eyes and to the practitioner for 'eyes on you'.

Building independence

In the first five or so years of their lives, children need to learn how to feed themselves, use the toilet, get dressed, do up their shoes, make friends, and so on. These self-care goals form a key part in children's development of self-regulation. Settings can play a vital part in supporting children to achieve these goals, by working with families to help their children become more independent. The skills that children learn during this time are very important for their later learning, because they allow children to become less reliant on adults to meet their daily needs. Learning independent behaviour is a gradual process, and the speed at which they can achieve this will vary from child to child. Those children who have had adverse experiences during their early years may attach themselves more strongly to adults for reassurance. Those children who have some types of special needs may struggle with independent tasks.

In order to support your children in learning to be independent:

✓ Think about which jobs in the setting could be done by someone other than the adults. Always consider whether you could get a child volunteer to do something before you do it yourself.

✓ Build routines into the day so that the children gradually learn how to take more responsibility.

✓ Put structures in place to support the children to behave independently and encourage parents to let their children do as much for themselves as they can.

✓ Use visual aids so that children can identify their own coat peg and hang up their own coats.

✓ Encourage your children to self-register by finding name labels and putting them on a registration board. They might register according to what drink they would like at snack time (e.g. milk or water), or they could register according to their mood (e.g. sad/ happy).

✓ Where space allows at drop-off or pick-up time, ask children to choose a new storybook or to change their reading book with the help of parents.

✓ Model independent behaviour for your children, taking things one step at a time. At first, you may need to help a child to find the right wellies and put them on the correct feet. Gradually, though, the child will be able to do more for themselves.

✓ Show the children how you do different tasks yourself, talking them through the process so they can copy you and learn the steps they need to take – for instance, getting dressed in an all-in-one suit for an outdoor learning session.

✓ Don't rush the process of learning independent skills. Set aside plenty of time for self-care activities such as putting on waterproof clothes for a forest school session. Getting dressed always takes more time than you think, and the temptation to intervene is always stronger if you are in a rush.

✓ Use lots of visual back-ups to help your children build their independence – for instance, having a matching image for each child's peg and book tray.

Toilet training needs to be very much a joint process, where the setting works together with the parents to support the child. Talk with parents about how they can support you in this, by ensuring that the child has spare clothes in case of an accident, for instance. Regularly discuss progress and plan for next steps.

Strategies for building independence

One of the keys to helping your children become more independent is to give them enough agency in their learning, and more generally in the setting, even if that means that sometimes they make poor choices or mistakes. If you always tell your children exactly what to do, and how to resolve the issues they face, they will never learn to persist and handle these struggles themselves. The struggle plays a key part in the learning.

In order to build independence:

✓ Try the 'three before me' approach, where you ask the children to try three things before coming to the practitioner or teacher for help. For instance, they could think again, ask a friend, or have a try at doing whatever it is by themselves.

✓ Involve the children in setting their own targets and goals. What do *they* want to learn today? Towards the end of the session, reflect on how they did in meeting their goals.

✓ Give the children plenty of time and opportunity to make independent choices – for instance, deciding on what resources they would like to have out on that day or where they want to play.

✓ Aim to highlight the process that children are undertaking rather than praising the outcome, as this helps to build their sense of confidence and control. For instance, rather than saying to a child, 'That's a brilliant painting', try saying, 'You are really getting the hang of painting now.'

✓ Spot a mistake in their work, but rather than telling them how to repair it, say, 'I know you can put this right' and then walk away, giving them plenty of time to try to put it right for themselves.

Chapter Five
Building Positive Relationships

In this chapter:

- ✓ Understand the power of attachments to support the learning of behaviours.

- ✓ Think about how to ensure smooth transitions into and out of your setting.

- ✓ Consider the role of the key person and how to develop it.

- ✓ Understand more about how children build relationships with their peers.

- ✓ Examine ways to help children build empathy and emotional intelligence.

- ✓ Think more about how to build supportive links with your families.

Positive relationships are very much at the heart of the early years, as settings work together with the children and families to support the care, learning and development of the children. All behaviour happens within a relationship: it is through forming attachments with both staff and other children that babies and children begin to feel 'at home' in our settings. Over time, these relationships can build into strong and often lasting attachments, which in turn can support the children in learning to self-regulate. They can also help the children's levels of attainment more generally. A child who is comfortable, confident and happy in your setting will be able to play and learn more readily. Where children and families view your setting as like a 'second home', they will be highly motivated to attend and connect with the work that you do, and children will be able to learn to regulate within the secure and trusting relationships that you have built.

The early years period is a very particular phase of education in terms of the relationships that are built within it. This is a non-compulsory phase: until the term after they turn five, children are not even required to be in full-time education, let alone in our settings. Early years practitioners are responsible, not only for the children's learning and development, but also for their care. In many ways, practitioners take on a role of caregiver that is very similar to the parental role. You might have heard people refer to the idea of 'professional love' – a concept developed by Dr Jools Page to describe the kind of relationships that practitioners build with their children.[4] Children in this age group need warm, supportive relationships that mirror the type of relationships that happen within a well-bonded family unit. The role of an early years educator is not solely that of a teacher, it is about the development of the whole and unique child.

Effective transitions

A key part of becoming independent is a successful transition for children from parents or carers and into an early years setting. An anxious or unsettled child is likely to display distressed behaviours. We want our children to be happy, settled and ready to play and learn. This means that effective transitions have a crucial role in helping children to self-regulate and in improving outcomes for the children. A child who is new to your setting needs time to settle in. At first, the child might appear introverted or withdrawn. However, this behaviour may change once he or she feels comfortable in the new environment. Move slowly during transitions: do not rush the child or insist that they play with others, or you risk exacerbating the situation. Think carefully as a staff team about how you are going to manage transitions. There are lots of questions to consider.

Reflection Activity

Work as a staff team to consider your approach to transition. How and where can you support the children in accessing and settling into your setting? Talk together about:

✓ how home visits are managed and what happens during these visits.

✓ which staff are responsible for which parts of the transition, and how staff work together to ensure a coherent approach to this.

✓ how you ensure that children are placed with the right key person for them.

✓ how you make sure that families feel confident to ask any questions they might have of the setting.

✓ the emotional impact on parents of leaving their babies and children in your care.

✓ what happens to the key person's group of children if a member of staff leaves the setting.

Remember to think about the transition *out of* the setting as well as into it, as the children move on to school or into a year 1 class from reception (in England). To ensure that the children take the behaviours they have learned with them, and settle quickly into the next part of their education, it works well to:

✓ Create ongoing links with the next setting or settings, so that the children feel familiar with them before they move.

✓ Set up 'joint ventures' with the settings that you feed into – for instance, taking your children to the school sports day and inviting them to yours, or taking the children to watch the school nativity play.

✓ Invite teachers into your setting from the feeder schools to meet the children and start to get to know them.

✓ Develop projects where the children use some of the same formats for learning as they will be using when they move on. For instance, in our setting we use Pie Corbett's 'Talk for Writing' storytelling approach, which is also used at the local primary schools. The primary children visit us to share their stories and we share ours with them. This creates a point of familiarity on transition.

Home visits

Home visits play an essential role in supporting children's transition into a setting. They allow you to start to form a relationship with the family, and they help the child and their parents get used to what the setting will be like. At the time of writing, the pandemic means that settings are having to undertake home visits virtually, and many practitioners are actually finding this a very useful addition to their toolkit. Most of the strategies listed below could be utilised in a virtual visit as well as in person.

To make the most of home visits:

✓ Take along some photos of staff and your setting to share with the family. You might like to make a book about 'Our Setting' to take with you.

✓ Consider bringing along some toys from your setting so that the child can play with them and become familiar with what might be on offer while you chat with parents.

✓ You could also share a list of the nursery rhymes that you use regularly in your setting so that the parent can sing these with their child at home.

✓ Support the family in completing any registration paperwork if they need your help.

✓ Provide materials in community languages where appropriate.

✓ Talk the parents through your daily routine and answer any questions they might have about your provision.

The settling in process

Some children adapt very easily to being in an early years setting: they settle quickly and do not seem overly concerned about being separated from their parents or carers. Other children, perhaps the majority, struggle somewhat with the initial separation, and some struggle so much that it becomes a source of anxiety for both the child and the parents. Remember that the anxieties that parents or carers feel can easily transmit themselves to the children, so aim to quell parental worries as well as thinking about what you can do for the children. I can well remember how difficult it was as a new mother to leave my own very young children at nursery, and how hard it was to hear their cries as I left. Practitioners should take steps to make the transition from the home to an early years setting as smooth as possible, especially for those children who find the separation process distressing.

To ensure a smooth transition:

✓ Focus on keeping both parent and child calm and relaxed. Where at all possible in the context of the setting or the parental situation, do not put pressure on them to separate if they are not comfortable doing so.

✓ Be clear with parents about your policy, ahead of the child starting. Some settings prefer a 'clean break' early on; others will accommodate parents who wish to stay with their child until they are both ready to separate.

✓ Let parents know that, although their children might appear upset as they leave the setting, they will typically settle quickly once the parent has gone.

✓ Be clear that you would *always* call or contact the parents if a child continued to be distraught and you could not settle them.

✓ Remember that distractions can work very well for young children who are upset. Comfort children to calm them down, then take their mind off the separation by offering something exciting to play with.

✓ Let the children bring a toy or comforter of their own into the setting so that they have something familiar that will remind them of home.

It is especially important in terms of building trust that parents do not 'sneak off' when they leave their child at your setting. Encourage them to wave goodbye and then move away confidently. If they are very anxious, they could wait outside and you could give them a progress update after ten minutes or so, to let them know that their child has settled.

The role of the key person

The 'key person' system is unique to the early years sector – a single member of staff acts 'in loco parentis' – literally becoming the key person in the setting for the child and their parents. The key person system plays a vital role in the child building an attachment to a key member of staff, and this in turn supports the child's development of self-regulation within that relationship. In our setting we have separated out the role of 'settling person' from 'key person' – our lead practitioner makes the initial contacts with the home and helps to settle the child in. Once this has happened, we find the right key person for the child and a handover is done.

The key person might do some or all of the following for their 'key children':

✓ Undertake a home visit for the child to make the initial contact.

✓ Help parents in completing any paperwork required to access the setting.

✓ Support the child during the settling in process.

✓ Be the main point of contact for parents if they have any concerns.

✓ Be responsible for observations of the child's learning and progress.

✓ Take the lead in planning for 'next steps' for the key child.

✓ Update the child's learning journey document or participate in any other form of tracking and assessment that the setting uses.

✓ Highlight any concerns that might arise about the child's development to the setting's SENDCO (Special Educational Needs and Disabilities Coordinator).

✓ Give daily/weekly feedback to the parents about what the child has been learning in the setting.

✓ Talk with parents about the child's progress at parent consultation meetings.

Thinking about socialisation

Just as there is a broader set of rules that govern our behaviour in society, so young children need to internalise what is effectively an unwritten set of rules about how we expect human beings to behave towards each other. If our children can grasp these unwritten rules, they will find it much easier to develop friendships and to play a positive part within their communities. It is interesting to consider what the key aspects of social behaviour and socialisation are that children need to learn. Your 'take' on this will depend a little bit on how you were brought up (or 'socialised') and the culture and type of society in which you live, but there are some general principles that hold true wherever you live.

People would generally agree that socialisation is about developing the ability to:

✓ share resources.

✓ wait and take our turn.

✓ make friends and be friendly.

✓ be kind to others.

✓ cooperate with others.

✓ be polite/have good manners.

This is all about learning what we might refer to as 'social norms' – the implicit agreements that are made within and across a society about how people 'normally behave'. This last concept, of 'politeness' and 'manners', is a very interesting one, because it is typically highly culturally specific. In some cultures or societies, a hand gesture can be considered rude, whereas in others it is considered acceptable. Another example is direct eye contact, which again is considered rude in the context of some cultures. It is important for practitioners to consider cultural differences when making judgements and statements about what is and is not polite.

Building social behaviours

One of the great benefits for young children of going to an early years setting is the opportunity to play and socialise with their peers. In fact, if you ask parents, they will often state this as one of the key reasons for sending their child to a setting. They want their children to learn to play with other people's children. Even those parents who do not have to use childcare in order to work will often choose to use some or all of their funded hours because they can see the social benefits for their child. Always keep in mind that you are responsible for the 'care, learning *and* development', not just the learning, of the child.

Healthy peer-group relationships are crucial for the children's development over time; the children are learning how to behave as a friend and how to form and maintain social relationships. As well as making friendships, the children will also be learning to get along within a community of learners – to work alongside and share with others, even if they are not actually friends with them. Learning to be cooperative and to form positive relationships will stand them in good stead both in school and in the world of work beyond. These positive relationships are very important for the mental health of children and young people.

Some of your children will appear to be naturally extroverted – they enjoy being at the centre of a group of other children and will have no issues about being in a busy environment full of people. Other children might prefer to be in a small group or to play on their own. This may be partly a result of early experiences in the home. For instance, a child who has been brought up in a large family with lots of siblings may find it easier to socialise than an only child from a single parent family.

Although it is perfectly possible to be introverted and to feel happy and confident, people do tend to equate outwardly expressed confidence with positive attitudes. Some children are naturally confident from a young age, and willingly take the lead during group play, with the other children happy to follow their lead. However, a confident manner within the peer group can sometimes tip over into bossiness and even aggression. Ideally, we want children to develop the key skills of both confidence and empathy: to learn how to play with their peers in an inclusive and friendly way rather than always feeling the need to be 'in charge'.

To support your children in building social behaviours:

✓ Remember that it can be harder for small children to play with members of their peer group than it is for them to play with adults. At this age, the other children are learning how to socialise as well, and some of them may struggle to play in an inclusive way. The adults play a key role in supporting gradual socialisation.

✓ Keep a close eye out for any children who seem isolated from the main peer group, who often play alone, or who try to enter the play of others but are rebuffed. You may need to offer these children extra support in learning to socialise and, depending on the specifics of the situation, you may also need to explore the possibility that the child has a special educational need.

✓ Involve practitioners in supporting the development of social behaviour by modelling 'good relationships' for the children. For instance, you can model what 'good sharing' looks like by demonstrating the sharing of a toy with another practitioner.

✓ Help a child who seems isolated from the peer group to join in with play by gently introducing the child into games or role plays. You might offer to go with the child to sit with the group and play, so that they will feel more confident about joining in.

✓ Be really clear about your expectations of behaviour around socialisation and sharing. Talk together about how and why we need to learn to share and respect other people's ideas. It is useful to have ideas about sharing and being kind within your golden rules.

✓ Think about the strategies you use to ensure that all the children can share their ideas when learning as a group – make it clear that you are looking for a fully inclusive approach, in which everyone's ideas are valued.

✓ Be clear that children should learn to listen to each other, and that they must give respectful comments about other children's suggestions. Be firm about disrespectful comments, insisting that 'we do not say those things in our setting'.

A good technique to reinforce the need for the respectful sharing of ideas is to focus all your attention on the child who is sharing their ideas. If someone interrupts, do not acknowledge the interruption, but simply ask the child who is speaking to pause. Then reiterate to the group that 'we respect each other's ideas' and ask the child to wait to restart until they are sure that everyone is listening properly.

Learning to share and take turns

Being able to share and take turns plays a crucial part in building relationships – we must learn not to be focused on our own needs being met over the needs of others. Children's ability to take turns and to share is closely linked to the development of self-regulation. In order to be able to wait for someone else to 'have their go', they have to put their own wishes to one side momentarily. They must understand that other people have feelings, just as strong as their own, and that it is a good thing to try to make other people feel happy and valued. Children also need to learn to regulate their reactions to someone else having something that they want, whether this is the teacher's attention or a particular toy, game or resource they want to play with. Those children who have very little in terms of resources at home, or who have faced a situation where resources are not reliably available to them, may struggle more with this than most.

There are lots of learning experiences that will help your children develop the skills of sharing and taking turns. Clearly, we cannot learn how to share on our own, so group play and activities are especially useful for the development of this particular set of behaviours. For instance, you could:

✓ Link the learning of turn-taking with the development of empathy by asking the children to talk as a group about why it is important to share. Ask them how they feel when someone refuses to share something; ask them how they feel when someone is happy to give them a turn.

✓ 'Show and tell' offers an early introduction to this concept, because the child shares something that feels important to them, and the other children are encouraged to acknowledge how and why they see it as important.

✓ Play group games in which the children have to share in order for the game to be successful – for instance, pass the parcel, parachute games or activities where the children have to pass an object around a circle.

✓ Children love the idea of 'beating the adults', so it can work well to try a game where the children work cooperatively against you.

✓ Play some small group games that encourage sharing and group interactions – for instance throwing and catching a ball. Create an incentive to share the ball equally around the circle. For example, the children have to sit down as soon as they have thrown the ball, so that everyone gets a turn.

✓ Where children are struggling to join in and share with larger groups of peers, aim to create situations where they can play with one or two other children to gradually build up their confidence in social situations.

Emotions and child development

In early childhood, children believe that they are the centre of their own universe, just like people used to believe that the earth was at the centre of the solar system. It's not that they are being rude, it's just that they are not able to put themselves 'into someone else's shoes'. They cannot yet conceptualise the idea that other people are separate entities, with their own hopes, wishes, dreams, emotions, and so on. Young children cannot yet understand that other people might feel differently to them, or even that others might feel the same as them. In their world view, their desires are the most important thing of all. It is the process of gradually learning to see other perspectives, and take account of them, that is a key part of development for this age group.

During the early years of their education (and in the years beyond as well), children need to develop an understanding of the idea that their own desires and wishes do not always come ahead of those of the group or community as a whole. While each of the children matters, no individual is more important than the group within which they live. This is the skill of empathy, and it is one that we all need to develop in order to work well within our wider society and for our wider society to be kind and inclusive. Where older children get in trouble for problematic behaviours in class, it is often the case that they seem to lack awareness of how their behaviour might make other people – including their teachers – feel.

Understanding emotions

We are not born understanding or being open to other people's emotions; it is a skill that develops during childhood. At first, we are mainly concerned with our own emotional state, but gradually we learn to become sensitive to other people's feelings. To do this, we need to accept that our view is not the only view, and also learn to position ourselves in a different way in order to see other perspectives. This is a particularly sensitive part of the work of an early years educator, because we do not want to make the children feel guilty or anxious about their emotions or the impact they have on the emotions of others. Tread carefully with any children who present as particularly nervous or who have SEND.

Take great care in the language you use around children's emotional states. Do not label emotions as 'negative'. There is nothing negative about expressing frustration, anger, upset, worry or anxiety. If children are taught to supress these emotions rather than learning to accept, handle and deal with them, it could potentially lead to issues with their mental health. It might also encourage children to hide the true nature of their emotions because they pick up the way the adults feel about their expression of emotions.

To help children in understanding their own emotional states:

✓ Use open-ended language when you are trying to figure out what is going on with a child – for instance, saying, 'Is there something I can do to help you?'.

✓ Help children to understand their own emotions by identifying the emotions you see in them – for instance, 'I can see that this has made you really upset.'

✓ Be open to talking about emotions, and fight the urge to 'shush' children when they are expressing an emotion you are not comfortable with. The aim is not to immediately stop or pause the emotion, but to help the child to learn to cope with feeling it.

✓ Encourage the children to think about, discuss and share the impact of both appropriate and inappropriate behaviours on other people's emotions. Ask: 'How does it make you feel when …?' You could do this in carpet time discussions or with small groups during their play.

✓ Ask the children to consider how other people's behaviour impacts on their own emotional state and that of others. For instance, if someone snatches a toy from them, acknowledge that this action may have arisen from, and given rise to, painful feelings in them – for instance, anger, irritation or upset.

✓ Phrase what you say to include lots of questions – for example, 'How do you think Ben felt when you took the toy away from him?' and, 'Ben, do you want to talk to Irena about how it made you feel when she did that?'

Talk to your children about the attributes and attitudes we need in order to build and maintain positive relationships. Ask questions such as:

✓ What makes a good friend?

✓ What does a good friend do for you?

✓ How could you make friends with someone?

✓ Why is it important to share and take turns?

✓ How can we help others to join in with our play if they are shy?

Reflecting on and helping children understand their emotional responses is all part of the development of self-regulation.

Building empathy

Empathy is all about understanding someone else's perspective and being able to see the world from different points of view – 'standing in someone else's shoes'. This is a surprisingly hard thing for people to learn to do. It is especially difficult when you are trying to see the perspective of someone with whom you don't agree, because of the way in which our own biases can make us struggle to accept any opposing views. When we support children in building empathy, we help them understand how their behaviour makes other people feel. This in turn supports them in their learning and in their self-regulation, because it helps them see why others might also want their own opinions and ideas recognised. It gives the children an understanding of why they need to wait for their turn in a whole-class discussion and to be supportive of other children's contributions, because they gain an understanding of *how it would feel for them* if they weren't.

Even as adults, we can find this idea difficult. We tend to push our own viewpoints to the front rather than stepping back and allowing other people the space to voice their own ideas. In order to help your children build empathy:

✓ Share stories with them about other people, the situations they faced, what they did in those situations, and how it felt for them. The stories you use can include biographies and autobiographies as well as fiction.

✓ Talk as often as you can with your children about the impact their behaviour has on other people and why it is important to be kind and to treat others as we would like to be treated ourselves.

✓ A really useful technique is to get staff to role play a scenario where one of them is being destructive of the other person's play. Talk with the children about how this kind of behaviour might have made the person feel. What could they have done to behave differently in this scenario?

✓ Give the children lots of opportunities to 'just imagine' – to go into their imaginations and to think about things that are separate from their own experiences. This might include role play, stories, nursery rhymes, and so on.

✓ Use an imaginative focus to help children learn behaviours by the application of empathy. For instance, when they are moving from one activity to another, ask them to imagine that there is a sleeping giant under the floor and that they must not wake him up because it would upset him. They must tiptoe as quietly as they can across the floor or else he might hear them.

✓ Literally get your children to 'walk in someone else's shoes' by offering them shoes and costumes that fit a range of characters and then asking them to imagine that they are the person. Children will often do this naturally. For instance, during superhero/heroine play, they understand that 'their character' is brave and can 'save the world'. You can adapt this to other roles – a vet, doctor or teacher, for example.

✓ Another great way to develop different perspectives is to ask your children to take on viewpoints that they don't agree with and try to make a case from that perspective. Arguing for something you don't believe is surprisingly tricky to do.

Sometimes children struggle to build empathy, and consequently to socialise, because they find it hard to read the verbal and non-verbal cues we give to show our moods. This can be the case for children who have an autistic spectrum condition (ASC). They may struggle to read the cues that others find easy to understand. You can support children in building this skill by looking closely at people's faces and talking about what their expressions might be 'saying'. You can also help individual children to 'read' how other children are feeling by talking about these cues in your setting. For instance, you might say, 'Oh, look! Jenna must be enjoying that game. She's smiling and laughing as she plays.'

Building relationships with children and families

An early iteration of the EYFS in England stated that 'parents are their children's first and most enduring educators'. It is through the basis of a relationship with their families that we build the best kind of care for the children who attend our settings. We need to see ourselves as working alongside the families to help the children develop, because this is the best approach for the children. Even those children who are in full-time day-care will still spend far more time at home than they do in a setting over the course of the year. This means that supporting families to support their children is critical in ensuring the best outcomes, and this includes supporting parents and carers to understand how to help their children in learning behaviours.

The stronger the relationship you have with your children, the more likely they are to pick up on and try the positive approaches you are trying to demonstrate. Where children see you as someone to look up to and emulate, they are more likely to model the behaviour they see. This can also apply to the way that parents see you interacting with their children. Aim to involve your children and their families in lots of different ways to show the children that you are all working together to learn. Help your families to set goals and targets for learning, as well as thinking about helping the children to set these for themselves.

For instance, you could:

✓ host a workshop in which you share and teach techniques for various parts of the curriculum – for instance, supporting children's reading at home or the best ways to set boundaries for behaviour.

✓ put ideas for home learning in a blog and ask parents to respond by sharing examples of what they have done at home.

✓ set achievable targets, along with the child's parents or carers, to ensure that you are all aiming for the same goal at the same speed.

✓ use WOW slips to increase home/setting communication – small slips of paper that you send home, with 'WOW' written on them, to encourage parents to note and praise what their children do at home.

✓ ask parents to fill in the slips with examples of kind, independent or self-regulated behaviour so that you can reinforce and praise what has happened at home.

Chapter Six
Playful Pedagogies

In this chapter:

✓ Consider play as an ethical and pedagogical imperative in the early years.

✓ Explore the ways that play-based learning can support self-regulation.

✓ Consider the balance between child-initiated and adult-initiated learning.

✓ Understand how and why it is so important to give agency to your children.

✓ Learn about the power of sustained shared thinking to develop learning.

It would be impossible – indeed unthinkable – to write a book about the early years without advocating for the crucial role of play in this phase. The building blocks for thinking about appropriate pedagogies for this age group simply must start with play-based learning. Not only is this a decision based on what evidence shows is best for the learning and development of young children, but it is also the only ethical decision in what is mainly a non-compulsory phase. We cannot and would not wish to push the children in our care into doing formal learning activities that they do not want to do. Not only would this be wrong professionally, but it is not what most parents look for from our provision. The EYFS is about the 'care, learning and development' of babies and children, with an emphasis on the caring and nurturing aspects of the role.

Play is the way in which young children make sense of their world – it is the way that they explore its possibilities and its limitations. Play is the way that children build peer group relationships and learn how to negotiate and resolve conflicts. Play is deeply interconnected to the development of symbolic thought and figurative language. It is through playful approaches to creative tasks that children build their confidence and technique within different art forms. Interestingly, the ability to be playful and to 'play with' ideas is highly prized in the adult world, because it leads to creative outcomes and can help us be innovative and develop new ideas that make people's lives better. Research has shown that play deprivation can have a significant impact on outcomes for children, particularly around their social and emotional development. This alone should be cause enough to celebrate its central role within the early years.

Play and ethical considerations

Play is very much the key vehicle for learning in a child's early years. Play is first and foremost the right of all children, and is enshrined as such in the United Nations Convention on the Rights of the Child (UNCRC). Article 3 of the UNCRC states that the best interests of the child must be a top priority in all decisions and actions that affect children. Article 12 explains that every child has the right to express their views, feelings and wishes in all matters affecting them, and to have their views considered and taken seriously. And Article 31 states that every child has the right to relax, play and take part in a wide range of cultural and artistic activities.[5]

Developmentally, socially and emotionally, it is in the best interests of babies and young children for the adults who care for them to play with them and to create an environment where they can play with their peers. Play supports children in building communication and learning language, as they interact with each other and with adults. It allows children to express their views, feelings and wishes. Play lets them find out more about their world and their place within it. Play also helps children to build the vital social connections and networks that will support their wellbeing now and in the future. Above all else, play is what brings joy to children and to childhood – it is through being engaged in playful experiences that children feel happy and become more confident. Where children are engaged in doing something that is of interest to them and that makes them feel happy, you are unlikely to experience any 'behaviour problems'. Play is about learning to engage with the very act of being a learner.

When we consider our ethical position, it is crucial to remember – as mentioned earlier – that the early years period is a non-compulsory phase of education. Children do not have to be in settings, and could just as easily be at home with their parents or carers at this time, if their financial position allowed. So, should parents choose not to send their child to an early years setting, there is absolutely no compulsion on them to formally educate their children while they are at home. Let the children play, in other words.

The power of play

As well as being an ethical necessity, play is enormously powerful as a vehicle for learning and development. It is through play that children take so many key developmental steps: building language and communication, developing core and fine motor strength, building balance and strength, learning how to cooperate and negotiate, understanding how to share, learning how to sustain focus and concentration, developing their symbolic thinking, and so on. Remember also that play allows children to maintain their attention – any practitioner or teacher who has ever tried to directly teach a group of small children will know just how difficult it is to keep their focus for any significant length of time. Purely on a practical level, play makes the most sense as the key pedagogical approach for this age group.

It is useful to think about the different areas of your provision and the kinds of behaviours that the children will be learning and developing while they are playing in them. For instance, they will be:

✓ learning about different perspectives by playing a character in a role play area.

✓ learning to share when taking it in turns to use a ride-on toy in an outdoor area.

✓ learning to express their emotions while making a piece of art.

✓ learning how to communicate when playing games with each other.

✓ learning to maintain focus when building a tower from blocks.

You can find lots more on the links between play, learning behaviours and the curriculum in the next chapter.

Play and self-regulation

Because play is the way that children instinctively interact with and learn about their world, it has some key benefits in terms of building self-regulation. Young children are much more likely to manage their own impulses, and to direct their attention for longer periods, when they are playing. Play gives them a sense of agency and control over what they are doing, and typically a feeling of enjoyment too. The learning essentially becomes a by-product of the engagement they feel with what they are doing. Many types of play require us to take on a 'can do' attitude – to have a go and to learn through trial, error and experimentation. When they are being playful, children will create challenges for themselves to solve, building their metacognitive powers as they think about what they are doing and how they can solve any problems that they encounter.

There are many examples of the way that play can support the development of self-regulation. For instance, using some of the features that were identified earlier in this book in the chapter on self-regulation, the children could be:

✓ controlling the impulse to get frustrated when they can't quite figure out how the toy they are playing with works.

✓ managing their emotional state and building social skills when their friends want to do something within a game that they don't really want to do.

✓ understanding more about how their behaviours make other children feel when they see how their peers react to them while they are playing together.

✓ planning how to approach a task, and setting themselves goals – for instance, trying to build the longest train track they can, or having a goal to build the tallest tower.

✓ deciding where to focus their attention – for instance, focusing in on a toy as they play with it, to see what it does, and filtering out the distractions around them.

✓ shifting their attention from one thing to another – for example, as they build a toy farm and multi-task between creating farm buildings and positioning animals.

✓ recalling information – for instance, remembering how a toy worked last time they used it, and building on what they recall to improve their skill.

✓ being persistent in trying to thread beads onto a string in order to make a bracelet for themselves.

As you can see, play is a very rich source for the development of all these different kinds of self-regulation skills.

Play and the role of the adult

The way that adults perceive and perform their roles within the children's play can actively help or hinder the children in learning behaviours. As we have seen earlier in this book, over-helping can be problematic in terms of developing self-regulation skills, because the child becomes more helpless rather than less. Our instinct as adults is to immediately want to support and advise a child, particularly if they are finding something difficult. However, to do so can stop the child from building their own ability to face challenges and to work out how to overcome them for themselves.

In her book *Interacting Or Interfering*,[6] Julie Fisher describes the subtle differences between interacting with the children to support and develop their play and learning and interfering with their play to the extent that it might overwhelm the child and reinforce the adult's agenda of what that play should be, should do or should look like. The balance between interacting and interfering is about knowing when to take a step back, when to be available to answer the child's questions or to support the play, and when to make a delicate intervention to help the child build on their thinking and learning. Fisher describes how the processes of accountability and ideas of 'effectiveness' can lead to adults becoming over-involved to the detriment of the children's learning. As Fisher says, it is all too easy to accidentally 'hijack' children's play with our own agendas.

A useful way to avoid this urge is to stop yourself from immediately trying to join in with play in order to 'enhance it'. Allow yourself to stand back for a moment and to simply notice what is going on. Really listen in to the children and what they are talking about as they play. Try to listen in order to *hear* rather than listening in order to find a reason or a motivation to step in and do something of your own. An interesting twist on this is when a child asks the adult to join the play and directs the adult in how they should join it. This is a really good sign of strong adult–child relationships in the setting.

Play and the role of peers

Of course, it is very easy for us to think solely about the adult perspective and to forget that it is often the children themselves who support each other's play, deepening and broadening the learning of various behaviours during that play. It is in the very nature of play for children to have a sense of 'working together' to overcome challenges, to find consensus, to build something together, and so on. By finding ways to negotiate their roles in play with their friends, children are building some hugely important social and emotional skills. Again, it is important for the adults not to step in and solve all the problems that occur for the children, because this closes up the space in which the children would be pushed to resolve those issues for themselves.

It is interesting to note how powerful mixed age groups can be for the learning of behaviours with and from peers. Older children can act as models of appropriate behaviours for the younger children and assist them in learning behaviours, while playing alongside the younger children means that older children build empathy and learn how to be kind and careful. It is interesting to note that these family groupings are increasingly being echoed when the children get older, with vertical tutor groups now becoming a feature in a number of secondary schools.

Child-initiated play and learning

Where learning arises out of play that the child has initiated themselves, this gives the child that crucial sense that they have control of themselves within the world. They deal with any struggle or challenge through choice, and they figure out how to do the things they want to do. This kind of play and learning is very powerful for the child's feelings of agency, because it becomes clear to them that what they think, what they want to do, and what they have to say are seen as being of value. This means that the behaviours they are learning during episodes they have initiated themselves can be very important for the development of self-regulation.

You will sometimes see the concern that if the children 'only ever do what they want' they will miss out on certain areas of learning that they do not choose to access. It is hard to gauge how true this is, especially given that children do not learn in isolation and the presence of their peers can act as a strong motivation for wider learning. It is also hard to gauge the truth of the statement because children in this age group are picking up learning from the adults around them all the time, and it is likely that those adults will model a wide range of competencies and interests to them.

To help children learn from self-initiated play, a skilful practitioner can boost learning as appropriate. This might be through both planning for continuous provision to ensure that the children play with a range of resources and in a range of ways, incorporating the children's interests to encourage them to play with certain resources, and in gently guiding the children towards those areas of learning that they might not otherwise choose to access. Of course, while the statutory curriculum says what children 'must learn', we should not forget the fact that this is a non-compulsory phase. At the heart of what 'must be done' for this age group lie the prime areas, which are fundamentally about the healthy development of the children.

Balanced pedagogies

Generally speaking, although play-based learning is the key pedagogical approach for this age group, thoughts about what play-based pedagogy might look like in the early years fall along a spectrum. At one end, there are play-based and child-initiated approaches, planning 'in the moment' in response to the children, and at the other end there are more formalised, adult-directed approaches to play and learning, where adults think ahead of time about which topics to cover and plan for playful ways to access these. In between the two ends of the spectrum are lots of things that we might recognise as forms of teaching – modelling, explaining, scaffolding, and so on.

In any setting, practitioners will move backwards and forwards along the spectrum between child- and adult-led play and learning during the course of the day. They will make choices about which is the most appropriate approach to use for a range of different reasons. At times, they will choose to step back and 'let the children play', while at other times they will step in to help direct the learning. Not everything that goes on in an early years setting has to involve play – for instance, helping the children understand how to perform a particular self-care task such as putting on a coat is probably best done at first by modelling and explaining it. However, at the same time, the children might have 'played at' this kind of activity during role play even if it was not explicitly designed to teach them 'how to put on your coat'.

The factors that determine where a practitioner will be working on the spectrum between child-led and adult-led activities will include:

→ the age or ages of the children.

→ the mix of age groups within the setting.

→ the type of setting.

→ the time of day.

→ the type of activity.

→ the philosophy of the practitioner.

→ the philosophy of the other staff.

→ the requirements of managers/leadership.

→ what the children are doing or learning about.

→ what the practitioner feels the children need at that particular moment.

→ the routine or timetable that the setting follows.

→ the area of learning that is being explored or developed.

→ the way the children respond to what the adults are doing.

→ the context of the families who use the setting.

→ the wishes of the families who use the setting.

→ the perceived or actual pressures of accountability.

→ pressures from external agencies, such as local authorities, Ofsted and the DfE (in England).

Generally speaking, the approach will become gradually more adult directed and formalised as the children get older. By the time children reach a reception class in England (when they are rising five), they would normally receive at least some direct teaching, usually in phonics and maths. It makes sense that the approach becomes more adult directed as the children get older, because children become more able to give adults their attention as they develop. It is also sensible because the demands of the school curriculum mean that the children need to learn some skills that are more easily taught via adult-directed approaches. The age at which these adult-directed methods become more prevalent depends a great deal on the way that the phase is conceptualised. In England, we tend to see more adult direction once children reach the age of four, while in many countries a more play-based and less formalised approach goes on for much longer – typically until the age of six or seven.

Sustained shared thinking

Sustained shared thinking describes a model of talking and a way of working with children as they play that helps them to build on their thinking. It is an example of an approach to teaching that develops the children's metacognition. In other words, it encourages children to think about their own thinking. This skill is closely linked to the development of self-regulation, which is effectively about encouraging children to think about their own behaviours. Sustained shared thinking requires adults who are expert at using talk, discussion and open-ended questions to draw out, develop and build on a child's ideas, and to support their communication skills and their thinking. It is akin to modelling out loud the thoughts that happen inside someone's head as they think, learn and make connections.

It is absolutely not the case that every single time a child is playing there needs to be an adult diving in to start 'doing' sustained shared thinking with them. This could potentially feel overpowering to the child, and it would not be particularly helpful for learning either. It is worth taking your cue from the children's behaviour: where you notice a child exploring something alone, for instance pouring water from one jug to another in the water tray, it might be a good time to step in and discuss what they are doing and thinking as they play and explore; or if a child starts talking to you about what they are doing, you could choose to build on that.

Sustained shared thinking involves:

✓ a 'serve and return' conversation where both child and adult contribute to the development of thinking.

✓ the use of open-ended questions to help the child build on their thinking and enhance their understanding.

✓ careful support from a skilful practitioner, to draw the child's ideas out in a way that is similar to thinking out loud.

✓ puzzling through and exploring something that is noticed in the child's play.

✓ playing together and learning lots along the way.

The use of sustained shared thinking by practitioners has a number of benefits for the children. It helps them develop confidence, because the practitioner supports them to 'build on' their ideas in a way that is very similar to co-regulation. It also gives them a sense of agency and control over their own learning and play: it is the child and the practitioner who are working together to develop understanding.

Chapter Seven
Thinking Curriculum

In this chapter:

- ✓ Think about what 'curriculum' means in the context of the early years.

- ✓ Consider links between the early years curriculum and learning behaviours.

- ✓ Examine ways of using children's interests to boost self-regulation.

- ✓ Explore the links between attention, focus and learning.

- ✓ Consider the role of stories and provocations in enhancing curriculum.

The early years curriculum and the behaviours of the children in an early years setting are inextricably linked. Depending on the part of the world in which you work, your early years curriculum might cover a different age range to that in England (where the EYFS runs from birth to age five), but the principles of early childhood education will usually be roughly the same. This is generally speaking a non-compulsory phase where the focus is on the care and overall development of the 'whole child' rather than solely on their academic learning. And there is far less focus on the single subject areas that we might encounter in a school curriculum, although in recent years we have seen literacy and mathematics given particular prominence and weight in the English early years curriculum.

Practitioners in the early years are charged with considering the care, learning and development of the children. This is not just about 'an education', but about meeting the wider needs of babies, toddlers and young children. Parents and carers will certainly have a view on what this care, learning and development should look like, especially as many of them will be paying for childcare during the first few years of their child's life. Ethically, in a non-compulsory phase that sits outside of formal schooling, it is only right that settings should start from the needs of the child and not the needs of the adults or the requirements of the system. Sometimes, though, it can be hard to push against the pressures from government and the demands of accountability.

A curriculum for behaviour

Curriculum is undergoing something of a renaissance in England at the moment, prompted at least partially by the government's 'knowledge' agenda, but also by specific changes to the Ofsted inspection framework that promote the idea of curriculum as central to an effective education. Substantial changes to the Ofsted framework were implemented with the justification that they were designed to stop schools 'gaming the system' by narrowing the curriculum in order to do well in accountability measures. Early years settings, including those that are not in schools, have been caught up in the general move towards 'what is in' the curriculum. This means that practitioners and teachers may need to become more confident about explaining what they believe an appropriate curriculum for the early years looks like, and about communicating their beliefs to others.

The 'prime areas' of the EYFS framework in England demonstrate just how central the learning of behaviours is to the concept of curriculum in early years settings. Although in schools curriculum is mainly about the academic subjects that we would recognise from our own schooldays, in the early years it is about the whole child. The 'core curriculum' or 'prime areas' in England cover the children's personal, social and emotional development, their physical development and their growing ability to communicate and use language. As we saw in the last chapter, the pedagogical choices that we make about how to approach the curriculum are inextricably linked with the way we conceptualise the phase.

When you are considering how to explain your 'curriculum' to a visitor, for instance an inspector, remember that the curriculum is not just about academic attainment. Nor is the curriculum solely about learning factual information, even if you concur with Ofsted's definition of learning as including 'a change in long-term memory'.[7] It could be argued that a curriculum that promotes sharing, confidence, resilience, self-expression, empathy and emotional intelligence is just as valuable as one that promotes the skills of reading, writing and mathematics.

Topics, themes and interests

For as long as I have been involved in early years, topics have been a point of debate for practitioners when talking about curriculum. Should we structure the learning across the year and introduce the children to new information by devising activities that fit under specific topics? Should we work via themes, perhaps, or use a curriculum that incorporates lots of calendar events and festivals? Should we follow the children's interests and plan 'in the moment' based on what we see them engaging with in their play? Should we use a 'provocation' to inspire the children's learning and work outwards from this? Or should we do a mixture of all of these?

There is no right or wrong answer to these questions – much will depend on the age group you are working with, the system you are working within, the expectations from the leadership team in your setting, your philosophy of early childhood education, the age of your children, the context in which you work, your level of confidence in how much control to hand over to your children, the kind of approach you prefer to take, or even on what parents expect from your setting. Certainly, a topic-based approach is seen more often with older children (in reception class in England) and of necessity it lends itself to a more adult-directed approach, because the adults are usually making the choices about the topic areas. Typical topic choices that you might see include 'All About Me', 'Autumn', 'Mini Beasts', 'Under the Sea' and 'People Who Help Us'.

Thinking about the learning of behaviours, it is useful to consider these choices in relation to how they might help the children build self-regulation and develop their social and emotional skills, as well as thinking about how you cover the curriculum more generally. Whatever choices you make around how you plan for and develop your curriculum, it is the act of reflection and self-evaluation that helps you become a more effective practitioner. Again, bear in mind that many practitioners will use a mix of approaches – for example, using festivals to structure the year while mainly building on the children's interests, or using topics but being happy to go off course when the children raise an interest of their own that they would like to explore.

Taking the two main categories – the 'interests-led' approach or the 'topic-based' approach, here are some of the potential advantages and disadvantages to consider and weigh up to help you reflect on the decisions you make about your own approach.

The interests-based approach – potential advantages

✓ It allows flexibility for the practitioners when all the children do not attend all the sessions. They don't have to worry about some children 'missing out' on some parts of the planned curriculum.

✓ It encourages a focus on the 'unique child', because you are starting from their interests and needs.

✓ It allows for depth of exploration based on how long the children demonstrate an interest in a topic.

✓ It encourages practitioners to really 'tune in' to what the children are saying and doing and to where their play is going.

✓ It offers the children a high level of agency and control, as they see the adults responding to their ideas and feelings about the curriculum.

The interests-based approach – potential disadvantages

✗ It may be more difficult for less experienced colleagues to understand how to build effectively on the children's interests.

✗ It can lead to concerns from leadership teams about whether following children's interests means limiting their horizons.

✗ It requires a high level of skill to build effectively on the children's interests.

✗ It may feel daunting to staff to take the leap into the unknown, and some staff may find it difficult to tune in to the children fully.

✗ It means that staff really need to think about the environment the children will need in order to follow their interests, and this may be difficult with limited resources.

The topic-based approach – potential advantages

✓ It can be a useful way to structure the year – for instance, by including festivals and other calendar events – and to gather resources through planning ahead.

✓ It ensures that you give the children access to the knowledge you want them to have.

✓ It can mean that you broaden the children's experience, especially if they have not had access to a wide range of experiences in their lives thus far.

✓ It can be useful for staff to have a starting point to work from, particularly where they are not particularly confident or experienced.

✓ It can help vocabulary learning, as children are introduced to new words that they might not otherwise have encountered.

The topic-based approach – potential disadvantages

✗ It may encourage staff to focus on 'coverage' of the material rather than depth of the learning.

✗ It may cause practitioners to sideline the children's interests, because a subject is being covered later in the year.

✗ It may be difficult to manage in a sessional setting, where not all the children are in all the sessions.

✗ It may be difficult for children to 'feed into' a topic until they have sufficient knowledge and experience of the subject.

✗ It may lead to less agency and control for the children, because it can encourage a mostly adult-led approach.

× It may lead to behaviour issues where the children are not particularly motivated by the topic being covered.

× It may cause a potential mismatch between what the children already know and what they are able to understand – for instance, a two-year-old 'doing fireworks' before bonfire night when they actually have no idea what fireworks are.

× It can lead to missing out on those accidental moments of wonder and discovery, because the staff are worried about 'getting back to' the topic.

The unique child

One of the key considerations when you are thinking about your curriculum is the idea of the 'unique child' that is so central to everything we do in early years. The idea behind the concept of the 'unique child' is that you plan for the care, needs and learning of individual children rather than for a class or group as you might do in a school. This means that each of your unique children will have different learning needs when it comes to developing their behaviours. While for some of them the focus might be on boosting confidence or developing socialisation, for others the needs will be around impulse control and being able to self-calm.

Whatever their age, the child brings a whole host of knowledge with them to the setting, and it is the job of practitioners to find out about and build on that knowledge. By seeing the child as having agency over their own learning and bringing their own thoughts and ideas to the setting, you create a climate in which the unique child is at the centre. The idea that children bring with them their own 'funds of knowledge' means we acknowledge that the child is unique – that no other child knows and has experienced the same things that they have. Perhaps they bring with them knowledge of another language, or of a different type of family unit. Maybe they bring with them knowledge of living in another country, or of an unusual pet. Where we can celebrate and build on each unique child's learning, we boost that feeling of agency and of the importance we place on them as individuals.

Building on children's interests

Building on children's interests can work well in developing a curriculum for them, and particularly in helping them to learn to self-regulate, because to do so acknowledges their agency in learning. You might do this in conjunction with topics or themes, as explained above, or as the main approach to practise within your setting. A real positive when it comes to learning behaviours is that, by starting from the children's interests, we harness a key motivational factor. The children already want to learn about and explore the things they demonstrate an interest in. The practitioner builds on what the children already know and can do, so that they learn more.

You might have come across the idea of 'flow' in learning, a theory first proposed by the Hungarian-American psychologist Mihaly Csíkszentmihályi.[8] The idea of 'flow' is that the learner becomes completely immersed in an activity that is of interest to them, and which is suitably challenging for their level of skill, to the exclusion of all distractions. Practitioners will often notice this in young children – their fascinations seem to lead to a deep focus on and interest in the strangest things. For instance, I once saw a two-year-old deeply engrossed in scooping out the flesh of a pumpkin, spending ages just scraping it out, occasionally tasting a small piece.

In a non-compulsory phase such as the early years, it could be argued that following the children's interests is an ethical approach, because it puts the children right at the heart of the learning. Not only can it develop their agency, but it also acknowledges their interest in a particular aspect of curriculum and respectfully considers how we might develop it. Considering children's interests also encourages us to consider how they think about and conceptualise their worlds – for instance, noticing their schemas in their play and how we might utilise and build on these. How might we support a child who has an enclosing schema (for example, adding boundaries to play areas (such as fences around animals or items inside a circular train track), playing with boxes, climbing into/creating small spaces, putting borders around pictures)?[9] Or another who wants to transport resources around the setting?

There can be some confusion about what is meant by 'using children's interests' in planning for continuous provision. This does not mean only ever doing things with the children that they are already interested in and never introducing them to anything new. Rather, it means considering how you can build on and widen the children's interests by developing their thinking about and understanding of whatever it is they are interested in. Typically, this requires the practitioners to provide time, space, resources and attention for the child. It can also be about how we utilise the motivation created by children's interests. To give an example, if a child was really keen on learning about dinosaurs, we might use that fascination to develop learning in many areas of the curriculum. So, if the child was playing with dinosaurs in the small world area, depending on the direction of the child's play, we could:

✓ get hold of some craft materials and work with the child to create a dinosaur environment for the small world area.

✓ discuss how long ago it was that dinosaurs lived and find out what the child already knows about fossils.

✓ count together to see how many dinosaurs we have in the small world area.

✓ sort the dinosaurs into different types – whether herbivores and carnivores or dinosaurs from different time periods.

✓ introduce new vocabulary around shape, size, texture, length, width, and so on.

✓ create some 'dinosaur sounds' together and perhaps even record a dinosaur soundtrack or make an animation together.

✓ look at 'top trumps' dinosaur cards together and ask the child to teach you some of the facts that they know about dinosaurs.

✓ add some books on dinosaurs to the small world area so that you can all read up on them.

To give some more examples on the always popular 'superhero' theme, we might:

✓ enhance a role play area around the children's interests in 'superheroes' by turning it into a 'superhero headquarters'.

✓ send the children a 'superhero message' asking for help with a special task.

✓ create a new superhero with the children and design a costume for them.

✓ use 'superhero germ busters' as a theme for dealing with hand hygiene.

Continuous provision, planning and behaviour

When you are thinking about planning, remember to keep learning behaviours in mind, as well as thinking about the different areas of learning. Consider not only which skills or facts the children could be learning during their play, but also the balance between different types of play and the opportunities that are being offered for things like learning to play cooperatively, working as a team, facing challenges, and so on. Look for opportunities within your planning to promote the expectations that make up your setting's golden rules. Remember too that, as well as helping you to teach behaviours and helping the children to learn them, the way in which you set out and run your continuous provision will impact on the behaviours of the children within it.

You might:

✓ Consider how the activities that you set up impact on overall noise levels and levels of excitement. Plan for a balance between exciting, noisy activities and calmer, quieter ones.

✓ Think about which activities might encourage the children to develop specific behaviours. Where are they most likely to play cooperatively, to build empathy, to learn to share?

✓ Where children need to develop their learning in these particular behaviours, consider how you might incorporate their interests into those areas to make it more likely that they will play in them.

✓ Find ways to pre-empt problems, thinking ahead about the resources and activities that are likely to work best for different children and which resources and activities might lead to problems.

✓ Change your continuous provision during the course of the day to better suit the children who are in different sessions.

✓ Add to or change the continuous provision over the course of the week, depending on which areas seem to be leading to most engagement and learning.

✓ Consider which resources are most appropriate for different age groups, and adapt your provision when different age groups are in the setting. For instance, in our setting the youngest children mostly attend only for the mornings, so we can put out additional resources more suitable for older children in the afternoons.

✓ Put out fewer resources so that the children are encouraged to play more creatively and inventively with those that are available.

✓ Think about using open-ended resources to encourage creative and lateral thinking – for instance, a big pile of large, empty cardboard boxes and some masking tape.

✓ Consider the opportunities for learning during social times, as well as during continuous provision. For instance, snack time offers a whole range of opportunities for learning. Consider the kind of social behaviours that can be promoted during these times, such as sharing, waiting your turn, thinking of others, and so on.

Talking about feelings

One great way that you can help children with the personal, social and emotional aspects of their development is to give them lots of opportunities to think and talk about their feelings. In this way, they can become more aware of their own internal reactions, and also become more conscious about how the other children feel. We can offer the children opportunities to talk about their feelings throughout the day as an integral part of the curriculum, whether this is simply in our interactions with them or at specific moments within a routine.

For instance, you could:

✓ ask the children to self-register to say what their mood is like that day – are they happy, sad, and so on?

✓ use a show and tell session to encourage the children to talk about the favourite toys they bring to the setting.

✓ discuss the children's favourite animal or foods during a carpet time session.

✓ discuss which toys or resources the children like best when using 'children's choice' in order to add to your continuous provision.

✓ have a routine at snack time where the children are asked about something they have enjoyed so far that day.

✓ encourage parents to complete WOW slips giving examples of a time their children have talked about their own feelings at home.

Learning to listen and focus

The ability to focus, pay attention and listen are key behaviours that you can help your children to build up over time. The curriculum acts as a basis for learning how to do this, particularly those parts of the curriculum that involve group activities where the children have to listen to each other or the practitioner leads the learning (for instance, when reading a story to the whole group). The ability to direct our attention to something specific, and to avoid being distracted from it, are key self-regulation skills. Young children will naturally focus on something if their attention is engaged by it – this is how they learn about and explore their world. However, once their attention wavers, it can be hard for them to bring it back and for adults to encourage them to continue to focus.

Learning to focus and pay attention is, of course, vital for learning in the longer term. As children get older and move through the next phases of education, they will be required to sit still and listen to their teachers for longer periods. If they have not yet learned to focus and concentrate, this will impede their academic progress and it may cause them to get into trouble in lessons. In the early years, children generally have short attention spans, and it is important for them to be physically active for healthy development. To an extent, asking them to sit still and listen for long periods of time is setting yourself up for trouble. You will need to be adaptable and to limit the amount of direct teaching or talk that you use, particularly for the younger end of this age group.

When you are thinking about children learning the behaviours required to focus and pay attention:

✓ Consider how long you are asking your children to be still, and whether this might be longer than is appropriate for their age and their concentration levels.

✓ Bear in mind that you can gradually build up children's focus over time. Just like any other skill, this needs practice in order to improve.

✓ If some children struggle to sit still and listen, that doesn't mean you can't challenge the rest of the group or class to do so, especially if you have an adult who can support individuals who are not able to stay focused for as long as their peers.

✓ There is no specific amount of time that every child should be able to sit still at any particular point. Instead, you will need to build up gradually, taking individual needs into account. However, a rough rule of thumb for concentration spans is about 'their age plus two' for any activity that requires the child to pay focused attention to something that an adult is directing.

✓ Story sessions are a great time for children to learn how to be still. There is something very calming about listening to an adult read a story to the group, which will help your children to settle and still themselves.

✓ Story time is one of the best times of day for developing the children's ability to focus, listen and imagine. When you tell the group or class a story, think carefully about how you can make it simpler for them to be able to direct their attention.

✓ Encourage your children to find a comfy position before story time starts. There is no need to insist they always sit up straight; some may find it easier to be still if they lie down.

✓ Use a quiet, soothing tone to help your children settle, calm themselves and focus in on the story.

✓ Talk over the rules around time spent on the carpet, especially that the children should keep their hands to themselves and not distract others.

✓ Sometimes, you can incorporate an interactive element to story sessions so that there is plenty going on to keep your children's interest. You might do this by asking the children to join in with some of the movements in the story – for instance, pretending to climb a tree like a character in the story.

✓ You can also use a 'statues' game to help children learn how to keep their bodies still. Do a countdown, and on the word 'freeze' ask all the children to freeze as still as a statue. Gradually build up the length of time you ask them to stay still. You might also have heard this game referred to as 'sleeping lions'.

Learning to wait

One of the key self-regulation skills is the ability to control our impulses and defer gratification – to learn to wait for things that we cannot have right away. Even as adults, we can find this difficult to achieve, but it is an impulse that we can improve with practice. There are lots of ways, from within the curriculum, that you can encourage children to learn to wait. It is those moments where they feel the impulse to 'go', or where they want something to happen immediately, but then are able to control that impulse and instead wait. Understanding that they have this ability is a very powerful learning point for young children.

To help your children learn to wait, you might:

✓ Use activities that create a delay between one part of the learning and another – for instance, growing fruit and vegetables is a powerful lesson in the need to wait. As they follow the progress of the plants they are growing, the children repeatedly have to learn to wait for the crops that are the eventual end result.

✓ Learning that takes place around festivals will often incorporate an element of waiting – for instance, we can probably all remember how long it felt as a child to wait until Christmas Day. By celebrating festivals and marking them as part of your setting's year, you are teaching children the importance of having something to look forward to.

✓ In our setting, we also play something called the 'ready, ready' game. At the end of carpet time, when the children are ready to go off and play in continuous provision, our practitioner says 'Ready, ready' and then the children have to wait for the signal to move. This happens a few times, with the practitioner saying, 'Not just yet' and the children having to pause at the command. Finally, the practitioner says, 'Time to play!' and the children can leave the carpet.

Incorporating these small moments of impulse control throughout the day can be very powerful for learning self-regulation – for instance, when the children wait to be served a snack by their peers at snack time or wait to take their turn in a game.

Outdoor learning and curriculum

The outdoors provides a rich source in terms of the children learning behaviours. As well as gaining knowledge and skills as they play outside, children will also be building resilience and will be learning how to cope with a range of challenges. This is perhaps especially so for settings that can use some kind of forest school provision, particularly where the children spend longer periods of time outside. Just a few examples of the way in which curriculum can interact with learning behaviours in an outdoor or forest area are that the children might be:

✓ learning self-care as they get ready to go out, by putting on waterproofs and boots.

✓ working as a team to take equipment to a forest area.

✓ demonstrating cooperative behaviours as they build dens together.

✓ showing resilience and building strength as they climb trees.

✓ making transient art with leaves, etc. and learning to deal with the transient aspect of this kind of activity – that it is temporary and won't still be there next week.

✓ thinking about safety and responsible behaviours when making fires.

✓ building towers out of twigs or pebbles and challenging themselves to see how high these can go.

✓ working cooperatively to build dams or to help each other get up muddy banks.

The role of stories

Stories are a powerful tool for learning, and particularly for thinking and learning about our own behaviours and those of other people. Stories allow us to position ourselves in other worlds, other situations and other characters – ones that may be outside our direct experience. Stories contain imaginary elements that require us to visualise something that doesn't exist. Consequently, stories are an extremely useful tool for building certain key behaviours, such as empathy and an understanding of different viewpoints and perspectives.

In order to empathise with other people, we need to be able to see the world from their perspective or viewpoint. A well-written story helps us do exactly this, particularly a story where we literally imagine ourselves in the position of the central character. Remember the following:

✓ Stories are a fantastic resource for building empathy, because they help children to understand other perspectives, other lives, other places and other viewpoints.

✓ Role play also supports the development of empathy because it encourages children to 'take on' other characters and to 'act as if' they are someone else. This in turn helps them to understand what it is like to think or feel differently to themselves.

✓ It is useful for children to participate in role plays based around what other people do and to talk about why these roles or jobs are important.

✓ You can help the children develop their role plays by offering them a range of different role play scenarios to play within. Domestic role play can be a very rich source of language and understanding, because the children have so much experience of the home environment. The children will often take on adult roles during role plays.

✓ Remember that not all stories have to be fictional ones – they can be biographical and autobiographical too. You might invite some visitors from different backgrounds in to talk to the children.

It is crucial to think about the diversity that the children encounter within the stories you use. Are they seeing a full range of different people, including ones who mirror their own experiences, as well as the experiences of others? Are they seeing people who look like themselves, and examples of all the different kinds of family units? Are they seeing people who have disabilities and who come from all kinds of different cultures and backgrounds?

Using provocations

Provocations are a brilliant way to encourage children's agency and open-ended thinking. A provocation is a very particular form of adult-initiated playfulness, whereby the adult sets up a situation or scenario that will 'provoke' the children's play, learning and thinking. In essence, a provocation is a type of story. The provocation offers a challenge to the children's thinking, as it requires them to work out a way to solve a problem or understand what is going on. If you think about the way you feel when you are presented with a quiz or a puzzle, that kind of sparking of curiosity is a very powerful motivator for learning.

The provocations you use to enhance and inspire your curriculum might be:

- ✓ a trip or a visit to somewhere interesting, for instance at the start of the year, which is then built on in the setting.

- ✓ a visit from someone to the setting – for example, our local fire brigade brought their fire engine to the preschool and allowed the children to hold the hose while they sprayed water.

- ✓ a resource or an item that you bring in – for instance, buying some unusual fruits from a local supermarket.

- ✓ a 'story' that you set up within your provision to provoke thinking – for instance, an animal that gets trapped in a tree or a spacecraft that crash-lands in your outdoor area.

- ✓ a collection of objects that the children can add to and explore – for example, in a 'cabinet of curiosities'.

Chapter Eight
Enabling Environments

In this chapter:

- ✓ Understand more about the influence of the environment on children's behaviour.

- ✓ Explore how an enabling environment can support all kinds of learning.

- ✓ Think about how and why a free-flow environment helps to build self-regulation.

- ✓ Examine the importance of outdoor learning for young children.

- ✓ Reflect on your setting environment and consider how you can improve it.

The environment that we live, work or learn in has a direct and sometimes quite profound impact on the way in which we behave when we are in that space. Not only does the environment affect our behaviour, but it can also impact strongly on our mood, which in turn will impact on our learning. Early years settings really do come in the full range of shapes and sizes – from a purpose-built private day-care nursery to a school reception class squashed into a Victorian building to a voluntary-run preschool playgroup running as a pack-away setting from a village or church hall to a childminder operating from their own home – there really is no 'typical environment' in the early years sector.

What is noticeable, though, is that early years practitioners are typically very good at working flexibly to make the most of the environment in which they work. It is also noteworthy that early years practitioners are typically pioneers within the education sector in terms of offering their children access to outdoor learning.

Sometimes, we underestimate the impact of the environment on the behaviours we see. Perhaps this is because we don't typically have a great deal of control over the teaching spaces that we work within. Although we can change the layout or the resources, we are typically stuck with the space or the room. Remember that your environment not only impacts on the children; it also impacts on you and the other staff who work within it. The idea from Reggio Emilia that the environment is the 'third teacher'[10] is an interesting concept to explore and will ring true for many early years practitioners. The environment can teach many positives, but also potentially some negatives. It is always worth bearing in mind that the outdoors provides an additional environment, and one that is often far more flexible, changeable and challenging than the indoor one.

Making the most of your environment

When you think about the impact of your environment on the children's ability to learn different behaviours, always consider the space from the viewpoint and perspective of the children. It sounds really obvious, but it's surprisingly easy to miss this point. A factor to remember when considering your environment is that it is easy to stop 'seeing' it when you are used to it. The familiar often gets taken for granted, and it is quite possible to overlook things that might seem really obvious to someone visiting for the first time. You may find it useful to look at the work of Elizabeth Jarman[11] in this field, particularly to learn more about how to make your environment conducive to effective communication.

Before the children arrive in your setting, take a moment to put yourself into the mindset of the children. Look around, walk around and consider how it would really feel to come into the space as a child, and what you might want to play with or explore first. You might do this as a staff team and then discuss what you note. If you work in a pack-away setting, you could do this more regularly, as your continuous provision and layout are likely to change to some extent each day. If your setting takes babies, it is useful (if likely to feel a little weird) to actually get down on the floor and crawl around the space, so that you genuinely get a feeling for what the experience of being in that environment is like.

When you look at the space to assess it, it is worth remembering the following:

✓ Children are much smaller than us, and so their eyeline is at a completely different level to ours.

✓ When both children and adults are in a space at the same time – as they may be at drop-off times – the children will be seeing the space through a sea of legs.

✓ Young children entering a setting will be encountering a lot of different sensory information that they need to process.

✓ As well as the obvious, such as new sights and people, children will be encountering new smells and noises they might not have experienced before.

✓ It is likely that most children are less able to filter out distractions than we are as adults.

✓ It may be particularly tricky for children to avoid sensory overload on their first few encounters with the setting and the space.

When we think about the environment in this way, it really is no wonder that some children find it hard to transition into an early years setting and that they might subsequently react by getting upset. Until they are used to the setting, and the familiar routine that happens within it, the new environment may feel like too much for their senses.

Reflection activity

Work as a staff team to consider your setting environment and the likely effect of the space on the children and their learning. Talk together about:

✓ the space generally and what staff feel about it.

✓ if you use free-flow, how you handle the practicalities of this between the indoor and outdoor spaces.

✓ how well you manage resources and ensure that the children can access them – what the balance of resources in your setting is like.

✓ whether you see any areas of your environment as being particularly problematic, especially in terms of the impact on the children's behaviour.

✓ what the children would say is their favourite part of your setting and why.

✓ what the staff would say is their favourite part of your setting and why.

✓ how you would describe the overall feel of your setting in a single word.

✓ if there was one area of your setting that you could change, which part that would be and how you would change it.

Analysing and improving your space

You might like to use a staff meeting or an In-Service Education and Training (INSET) day to really dig down into what your environment is like and how you could improve it. Try to think 'outside the box' when it comes to the possibilities, because a lot of early years settings are based in spaces that are not purpose built, or in spaces that are shared with other users. This means that we need to become particularly skilled at adapting and working with what we have in order to improve our provision. Consider how to make what seems impossible a possibility. Try not to allow talk of difficulties to derail you; it is usually possible to make the most of a bad situation if you think laterally about it.

For instance, in our setting we turned a patch of scruffy, unused ground alongside the village hall into a garden, including a mud kitchen and a pond. Each day, we also turn part of the car park into our outdoor area by using temporary barriers. When the idea of becoming free-flow was first mooted, there was lots of talk about how difficult or indeed impossible it would be, but by adopting a bit of lateral thinking it has turned out to be perfectly feasible. We faced a similar situation when developing our forest club, as we have no handy forest nearby. Instead, we have ended up using a patch of overgrown and unused land that one of our neighbours loans to us, and we have gradually developed it with the children in mind. All these changes have had a direct impact on how the children learn behaviours while they are with us: you really can improve behaviour through changing the spaces and the environment.

When you are analysing your space, consider the following aspects of your provision:

✓ The space itself – what are the benefits and positives? How can you capitalise on these? For instance, it might be that your setting benefits from lots of natural light, and that you feel this supports the children's wellbeing because it creates an airy atmosphere. You might be able to utilise the light in some way – for instance, to create atmospheric displays or to do some activities based on thinking about shadows.

✓ The negatives or difficulties of the space, and what you might do or already be doing to overcome these. For instance, is there a pillar in an awkward spot? Instead of viewing it as a problem, have you utilised it as a feature? We use a pillar that gets in the way in our setting as a handy space to put up a key person display.

✓ Similarly, building on your thinking about the light in your setting, consider the kind of artificial light that is used, and how and when children might end up having to look directly into it – for instance, when their nappy is being changed – consequently becoming unsettled or upset. How might you adapt the space to resolve this issue?

✓ Which parts of the space remain constant, similar and familiar for the children and why you have chosen those particular parts and/or areas of learning. For instance, settings will typically keep one specific area for literacy learning, with a book corner or reading corner. Have a talk about this and about what might happen if you tried having a completely different area as your 'same each time space'.

✓ How you would describe the atmosphere of your setting and whether this is intentional. Does your setting feel very 'busy' or is it quite 'zen', and why do you feel like this about it? The specific atmosphere of a setting is made up of a multitude of considerations – the staffing, the pedagogy, the space itself, etc.

✓ Young children, and those children who are unsettled for whatever reason, often like to snuggle into a small 'hidey-hole'. Are there spaces in your environment where the children can go to hide? If not, look to create some.

✓ The reaction of the children to what your space is like, in terms of their behaviours within it. What would you say are the typical space-related issues that you encounter? For instance, in a large open environment, you might have problems with behaviours such as children racing around the space in a dangerous manner. Conversely, in a small, enclosed environment, your issues might be more to do with behaviours expressing the children's frustration at the lack of opportunity to let off steam physically.

✓ What the outdoor spaces are like and how you make the most of these. How much access to the outdoors do children have? How do staff feel about working outdoors, or about the setting using a free-flow approach? If we are totally honest, sometimes the barrier to outdoor learning has more to do with staff attitudes than with children's needs.

Thinking about displays

We tend to think of displays as an intrinsic part of any educational environment. Certainly, they can brighten up a space, lifting the mood of staff and children and perhaps in turn improving behaviours. Similarly, displays can be a good way to communicate information to your children and your families. However, it is also the case that sometimes we use displays without really thinking through the practicalities and the implications for learning and behaviour. Considering the role of the environment as a 'third teacher', it is useful to take some time to discuss and reflect on your use of displays.

Think about the following points:

✓ The height of displays. For instance, if you want the children to stick their names on a display board to self-register, then it obviously needs to be at the height of the children and not the adults.

✓ How clear signs are for parents and carers. For instance, how you communicate the different roles that staff take on in supporting the children, such as key person roles, needs to be clear.

✓ How you make displays fully inclusive. For instance, how do you utilise any community languages that your parents and children speak within the displays that you put up for your families?

✓ How much parents actually interact with the displays you put up, and whether you can highlight them in some way to encourage active interaction with them.

✓ Whether displays can become cluttered. It is always a temptation to get lots of material across to parents at one time. Generally speaking, however, a cluttered display is a mistake and is less likely to be accessed.

✓ Think carefully about any displays that are used to highlight behaviour – for instance, the weather/traffic light charts that seem to be in fairly common usage in schools or the sticker charts with a 'race' to gain the most stars. We don't use any of these in our setting, and I would advise against using them to manage behaviour because of the potential to cause feelings of shame in the children.

✓ Consider how the children feel about a judgement on either their work or their behaviour being shared in public, particularly those children who might be struggling with this. Ensure that you ask the children's permission to display their work.

If you are in a shared space, as is the case for a considerable number of early years settings, you will have to think very carefully about displays. You may need to consider questions around data protection where the displays have any identifying features and take these down when you are not in session. You might also be required to remove all displays when you pack away, which can have an impact on whether or not you are able to spare the time to display things. Where you do have temporary displays, it can be helpful to use washing lines to peg up displays, or to use large felt-covered noticeboards. This way you can take down the whole line or board at once to store it when you are not in session.

Thinking about layout

Where we are encountering what we might perceive as 'behaviour problems', sometimes what we are seeing is a feature of the way that the children are interacting with the environment that has been created by the practitioners. Often, the issues that we notice can actually be resolved – either partially or completely – by considering how we might adapt the environment to work better for the children. For instance, if the children enter the setting and start racing around it, it could be that they perceive it as a 'free' and 'open' space where these behaviours seem appropriate to them. Some simple adaptations to the space should make it impossible for them to behave in this way in the first place, thus helping you avoid that 'behaviour issue' from ever occurring.

When you are thinking about the layout of your space, you may find it useful to consider the following:

- ✓ How you might use temporary screens to divide spaces in an open environment.

- ✓ How you could mark out different areas using different types of flooring.

- ✓ In a cramped environment, where the potential is for resources to get knocked over or damaged as children pass them.

- ✓ How easy children and adults will find it to move into and around the space.

- ✓ How children might be involved in, and given agency over, the layout of the environment.

- ✓ Whether the way you have laid out your environment could 'channel' certain impulses or behaviours in either a negative or a positive way.

Remember that the layout of the environment can be significant in making your setting more or less inclusive. For instance, if you have a child with a visual impairment attending your setting, how does the layout support that child in finding their way around independently?

Environment, self-regulation and routines

Think carefully about how the way you have set up your environment supports the children in accessing your routines. The more easily they can access the environment, the more independent they can be around your routines and the more they will develop self-regulation of their behaviours. A great rule of thumb on how inclusive and accessible your environment is, is to ask yourself how much of the daily routine your children can do without much (or any) adult assistance. Even with the youngest children, it should be possible for them to have a large amount of agency and independence when following the agreed setting routines.

When you are thinking about how your environment can support agency and independence, and consequently promote self-regulation, it is useful to consider:

✓ Consistent signage between different parts of your setting to help with the children's understanding of communication. For instance, ask the children to choose a picture that starts with the same letter as their name (e.g. a ball for Bilal). This picture can then be used on book trays, coat pegs, name labels for self-registration, and so on.

✓ How involved the children are in managing their own behaviours around the space – how often they are part of managing the routine for their learning community as a whole. For instance, as mentioned previously, the bell that one of our children rings in the morning when it is time for the group carpet session, to bring everyone together. Handing this job over to a child volunteer builds the children's confidence and offers the children a way to have agency within their peer group.

✓ How the children can get involved in accessing resources and choosing which ones they want to play with. You might, for instance, have a 'children's choice' time, where one of the children can go with you to choose a toy or resource from the cupboard. If this is not possible, you might create a 'children's choice' book that they can flick through to choose additional resources.

✓ How the children get involved in routines during the day, to build up their independence and encourage responsible behaviours and the development of self-care skills. For example, how do the children get involved in the preparation of snacks?

The free-flow environment

One of the joys of an early years setting is the amount of freedom and choice the children have about where they play and learn and what they play and learn with. Giving children autonomy over their own learning and decision-making is vital in order for them to build self-regulation. A 'free-flow' approach also allows children to develop their metacognition, because it asks that they make decisions about their own learning throughout the day. They are thinking about their own thinking and playing as they move around the setting and considering where they want to go next. In addition, free-flow requires the children to become more independent in terms of their self-care – for example, when getting ready to go outside and knowing what to do when they come back in.

Being able to offer free-flow for part or all of the day offers a lot of valuable opportunities for learning behaviours. For instance, the children might be:

✓ discussing and negotiating with their peers about where they want their play to take place.

✓ thinking about which resources are available to them in different parts of the setting and making choices based on that knowledge.

✓ learning more about what constitutes 'appropriate clothing' for different situations.

✓ becoming more aware of their own physiological state – for instance, understanding when they feel cold and need to put on more clothing.

✓ putting on coats and boots independently so that they can go outside on a cold or wet day.

✓ taking off coats and boots independently and putting them back in the right places.

✓ following hygiene practices, such as washing hands when they come in from outside or, as is especially the case at present, washing hands very regularly during the day for the purposes of infection control.

Outdoor environments

The outdoors is, of course, the perfect place for children to learn a wide range of important behaviours, and the levels of challenge provided by an outdoor environment are highly beneficial for children's learning. Playing outside also offers children important health benefits – from the need for sunlight to produce vitamin D to the need for strenuous physical activity to build muscle tone and strength. Being outside has been shown to benefit people's mental health. It boosts serotonin, the 'feel-good' hormone, and the natural world can also create a sense of calm in us. The outdoors really is a key 'enabling environment' for everyone, and particularly for children in the early years.

Some of the self-regulated behaviours that are learned outdoors include:

✓ building resilience in the face of adversity – for instance, learning to be able to cope with being a bit uncomfortable when they get wet or if they sting themselves on nettles.

✓ taking turns, waiting and sharing – for example, waiting to use one of the ride-on toys.

✓ learning to assess and manage risk – for instance, children thinking about which trees are safe to climb with the support of the adults.

✓ coping when they are upset or hurt – for instance, building the ability to self-soothe if they fall off a bike.

✓ supporting friends and peers where they get upset or are finding it challenging to be in the outdoor environment.

✓ having and holding to a clear set of 'ground rules' for playing and learning outside, to ensure everyone's safety – for instance, we have a clearly structured set of rules around how children are asked to carry a stick if they move around with it when in the forest area.

✓ planning for and undertaking challenges – for instance, setting up a marble run or water run, or building a large tower with friends.

Chapter Nine
Case Studies

In this chapter:

- ✓ Examine some of the most common behaviours seen in early years settings.

- ✓ Think about what these behaviours might be communicating.

- ✓ Explore ways to deal with these behaviours by looking at real-life examples.

- ✓ Understand more about how to help your staff deal with problematic behaviours.

- ✓ Consider how to support your families in dealing with these issues at home.

In this final chapter, you can find a series of case studies that examine various commonly experienced issues with children's behaviour in an early years setting and what might be done to resolve them. For each case study, you can find a description of some of the factors that are common to this particular issue, some clues and cues to look out for to help you identify what is going on, and some strategies and solutions to try in your setting and to pass on to parents. You might like to use these case studies to help you identify what your children's behaviour might be communicating to you and how you can help them to progress past these problems.

Case study: Over-tiredness

What's the issue?

Young children's sleep patterns can be disrupted for a range of reasons. It might be to do with lack of boundaries/routines for bedtimes at home. However, many parents simply struggle to get into a pattern or routine for getting their children to bed because of other pressures in their lives. Sleep deprivation in adults can compound the problem, because it makes it harder for parents to make the best decisions about what to do. Over-tiredness is a problem for children (and indeed adults) because:

✓ lack of sleep has a powerful effect on human beings.

✓ tiredness can alter mood.

✓ tiredness can lead to a drop in cognitive function.

It is easy not to identify over-tiredness as the problem, and our tiredness can lead us to misidentify the issue that is causing the way we feel. For instance, a baby who you thought was giving a 'hungry cry' subsequently falls asleep in the middle of a feed. The soothing effect of feeding has allowed the baby to get itself to sleep, but it was sleep that the baby needed rather than food.

Cues and clues

✓ Children in your setting appear to get increasingly irritable, upset and difficult as playtime approaches.

✓ You notice that behaviour gets more difficult in the periods leading up to playtime, snack time or lunchtime.

✓ Behaviour is always more challenging in the afternoons.

✓ Children regularly doze off when you are reading them a story.

✓ Parents advise you that their child normally has a nap in the afternoon on days when they are not in your setting.

✓ Parents tell you how exhausted their child is when they get home on days when they are at your setting.

Strategies and solutions

- ✓ Talk with parents about how they would like to handle a naptime for their child during the setting day, if appropriate.

- ✓ Factor in a nap-time for children where needed, creating a separate space, or secluded area, where they can go to sleep.

- ✓ Look at your overall timetable and consider whether you are giving the children sufficient opportunities for quiet time or downtime.

- ✓ Incorporate calming activities into your afternoon routine.

- ✓ Create a separate calm zone or quiet space in your setting – for instance, by using a sheet, room divider or tent.

- ✓ Older children within the age group might benefit from a period of meditation or mindfulness rather than a nap, in order to refocus and re-energise.

- ✓ In a reception class, look at your timetable across the day and week as a whole. Consider the possibility of moving around the timetabling of different subjects in order to accommodate the children's needs.

- ✓ Think carefully about when you incorporate any adult-led sessions, in order to maximise focus and attention and minimise tiredness.

- ✓ Use a game of 'sleeping lions' (where the children lie down on a carpet for a quiet period) to incorporate some rest without necessarily having a nap.

Working with families

- ✓ Give advice to families about getting their children into good sleep patterns. It is obviously preferable for children not to arrive at the setting in a tired or fractious mood.

- ✓ Check with individual families to see whether they need personalised support in terms of getting into a good routine around their child's sleep.

- ✓ Encourage parents to ensure that children spend sufficient time away from any screens in the period leading up to bedtime – half an hour is the absolute minimum.

✓ Similarly, encourage parents to create a calm, quiet atmosphere in the lead-up to sleep. Blackout curtains, low lighting and soft music can all be helpful.

✓ Suggest that a lovely way to aid your child's sleep is to share a story together. This obviously also supports literacy.

✓ Explain to parents that they don't need to wait until a child can understand a story to read to them. Sharing stories should start right from birth.

✓ Advise that a warm bath and a drink can help a child 'wind down' as they approach bedtime.

✓ Often, getting a child to sleep is a matter of calm repetition and persistence. Every time the child tries to get back up again, the adult should gently pop them back in bed and say, 'Time for sleep'.

Case study: Hunger

What's the issue?

Children's behaviour is very closely linked to their physical state. When children are hungry, you will often see difficult behaviours coming to the fore, as the children find it harder to control their impulses and their emotional state.

✓ As our bodies use up the energy from the food we have eaten, our blood sugar levels drop.

✓ Low blood sugar levels can lead to various issues, including dizziness, irritability and tiredness.

✓ Children are very active and burn up the calories they eat more quickly than do adults.

✓ Children are not so conscious of what their bodies are telling them and might not realise that they are hungry.

✓ Where children are focused on playing, they might miss the signs that it is time to eat.

In addition to these fairly standard issues around children's behaviours when they are hungry, there are obviously issues around food poverty and children living in poverty that are sadly all too common in the UK at the present time.

Cues and clues

- Behaviour in your setting regularly starts to decline just before snack time or lunchtime.

- Children (and staff) get fractious and irritable at the same times of day, without any obvious cause.

- Children arrive at your setting very early in the morning, perhaps without time to have had breakfast.

- The children rush to snack time and snatch at food as though they are particularly hungry.

Strategies and solutions

- ✓ Consider bringing snack time and lunchtime forward a little bit within your daily routine.

- ✓ Where you use a 'rolling snack' (where children can access a snack whenever they feel ready), make sure that you remind them regularly that it is an option to go and choose a snack.

- ✓ Perhaps note when and how often children visit your 'rolling snack' option to check who uses it, how often, and whether any children do not remember to take a snack.

- ✓ Consider offering more filling options at snack times. Include something carbohydrate- or dairy-based as well as fruit and vegetables. Dried fruit is also great for sustaining children's energy for longer periods of time.

- ✓ Have a plan for what you will do if some children finish eating their snack or lunch quicker than others and want to go off to play.

- ✓ Talk about this as a staff team. Is it essential that everyone finishes at the same time? Some children simply eat more slowly than others or prefer to take their time with eating.

- ✓ If some children feel that others are waiting for them to finish, do they perhaps not eat as much as they would if allowed to take their time?

✓ Do an activity where you look at lunch boxes and identify foods from the different food groups.

✓ Talk about the idea of 'five a day' for fruit and vegetables and look at the 'eat well' plate to see what a balanced diet looks like.

Working with families

✓ Have a chat with parents about any individuals who often seem to have behaviour problems when they are hungry. What kind of breakfast do they eat and how much do they eat of it?

✓ Encourage parents to send in a balanced packed lunch by suggesting items for each of the food groups.

✓ If your setting does not currently offer a 'breakfast club' option, you might consider adding this to your day to support parents who start work early.

✓ It could be helpful to suggest to parents that they set up the breakfast table the night before if they have to leave early and are in a rush.

✓ You could do a workshop for parents who are worried about their children's eating and give advice on developing appropriate eating habits.

✓ One very useful idea for parents is that, if they find it difficult to get their child to eat, they should offer lots of small pieces of food. They could cut up bits of fruit and small pieces of bread and let the child eat these as they wish.

✓ Explain to parents not to put pressure on children about eating, as this is likely to backfire.

✓ Where parents model good eating habits, this helps the child to learn. Encourage parents to try to make time for at least some family meals during the week.

Case study: Problematic language

What's the issue?

It's not all that unusual to hear young children using words that you would hope they didn't know, let alone that they would think to use. Unfortunately, this is one of those situations where what is modelled gets repeated.

✓ Children model the language they hear.

✓ Children may bring problematic language that is modelled at home into the setting. This might be about the use of swear words, or it might also be about a child who speaks unkindly to others.

✓ Children need to learn to be able to 'code switch' – to use language that is appropriate to different situations. By modelling these 'code switches', practitioners help children to learn what is and is not socially acceptable in various contexts.

It can actually be slightly amusing for adults when children swear, because it looks so odd coming 'out of the mouths of babes'. However, it's important that you don't let your instinctive reactions show, as this might reinforce the problem and encourage the child to swear again.

Cues and clues

✓ It's often the case that parents don't really understand how much their young children will pick up on the language that they hear around them – both the vocabulary they use, but also the intent of the words and phrasing.

✓ This can also be a peer group issue. In an early years setting where there are also older children around (a primary school or all-through school), children may hear words that they don't understand but that they do know get a reaction.

✓ Similarly, in a household where there are much older siblings or relatives, the child might be hearing these words spoken frequently.

✓ Some children will use swear words as a way of gaining adult attention. This is probably because they have seen how this language gets a reaction at home.

✓ Sometimes children just don't understand how their own behaviour affects others. An issue with empathy can mean that they just don't see the problem.

✓ It can also be the case that the child is using the inappropriate language to cover up for their embarrassment about something, or to explore a particular issue. For instance, during toilet training, a child might start to use a lot of words associated with toileting. These words might not be typical in 'polite society' but might simply indicate a child who is exploring the topic.

✓ It can be useful to tune in to the language that parents use when they drop off and pick up the children from your setting. Do you notice that they speak as though they don't realise the children might be listening in and picking up on what they say?

Strategies and solutions

✓ As a staff team, discuss how you are going to react and respond when a child uses inappropriate language.

✓ Decide together on a consistent approach that will be used by all members of staff at your setting. Make sure that the children receive the same reaction to the same language from everyone. For instance, you might decide that the most appropriate response is to ask the child to step to one side for a moment and then discuss with them why the language is not okay.

✓ Where a child seems to be swearing to get a reaction, it is important for staff to respond calmly. The more children gain attention for inappropriate language, the more likely it is that they will repeat the behaviour to receive the reaction.

✓ Encourage staff to talk to the individual to help them understand why these words are inappropriate and not to be used in your setting. Ask the child to think about how the other children and the adults feel when they say these things.

✓ If you do identify attention-seeking as the issue, it is useful to get all staff to focus on praising the child when they behave well rather than only giving them attention when they use inappropriate language.

✓ Talk to children about other ways they can express their frustrations – for instance, they could walk away from a child who is upsetting them or talk to their key person about how they feel.

✓ Help your children learn different ways to stop themselves from reacting instantly when they get frustrated – for instance, counting to ten or breathing deeply.

✓ It can also be useful more generally to talk with all your children about how we use 'kind words' and how we make sure we do not say anything that might upset someone else.

If inappropriate language is a big issue for your setting, you might consider having a golden rule about the expectation to use 'kind words'.

Working with families

✓ Talk to the child's parents about what is happening and whether there might be something going on at home that is causing it. For instance, is the child hearing these words from an older sibling, and could they have a word with the older child? (This can also be a handy way to avoid the parents feeling that you are accusing them of swearing in front of their child.)

✓ Ask parents whether they think the child's use of inappropriate language could be linked to something in the home. Perhaps the child is uneasy about using the toilet in your setting and is trying to cover up for embarrassment?

✓ You might suggest to parents that they could use a star chart or a WOW slip to reward the child for each day they manage not to use any rude words.

Case study: Excessive noise

What's the issue?

Research has demonstrated that what we call 'noise pollution' is a significant factor in outcomes for children. Where children live in homes on a busy road, it is not just the air pollution that is an issue – the pollution caused by noise can affect them as well.

✓ Rising noise levels can be an indicator of various issues, but also of some more positive factors with this age group – for instance, that the children are excited and engaged in learning.

✓ A noisy setting can be stressful for both staff and children. Quieter children may find it particularly difficult to cope with noise all day.

✓ Excessive noise can interfere with learning, as it makes it harder for children to concentrate, and this can particularly be an issue around language learning.

✓ There is a balance required between plenty of talk and periods of quiet and calm.

Our settings need to be places where there is at least some time for quiet, still, inward-looking reflection as well as the noise and excitement of busy, physical play.

Cues and clues

✓ Staff regularly complain about having a headache, especially at the end of the day.

✓ You often hear staff talking more and more loudly as the overall noise levels in the setting increase.

✓ Staff voices betray the fact that their stress levels are building as the noise level increases, because they sound increasingly high-pitched or stressed.

✓ There seem to be particular areas within your setting where noise levels are higher and this appears to be associated with particular activities.

✓ You regularly struggle to hear the children when you are talking one-to-one with them.

✓ The noise levels are very similar indoors and outdoors.

Strategies and solutions

✓ A certain level of noise is important. It shows that the children are engaged in their learning. This means that it is worth reflecting on where and when the noise occurs.

✓ Consider whether the high levels of noise happen at certain times of the day or all the time. This will help you work out whether they are linked to the children getting naturally excited or whether there is a general lack of control over noise in your setting.

✓ Think about whether the noise levels are higher when children move from one activity to another. If this is the case, it may be useful to focus on strategies for how they travel around the space.

✓ Consider who is making the noise, to figure out whether a group approach or an individual intervention will be more useful. Do some children make most of the noise or are all the children being equally loud?

✓ Have a golden rule about noise levels in different situations so that the expectation is clear.

✓ Observe how loud the staff are when they talk. They should be modelling the noise levels they want the children to achieve rather than raising their voices above them.

✓ It may be that some staff training on voice usage would be useful for staff to learn more about regulating their volume levels and best practice in voice usage.

✓ Consider the layout of your space and whether there might be something about the way the room is set up that is affecting the noise levels.

✓ Highlight children when you see them managing their own noise levels, and pinpoint this as a positive behaviour that you are looking for.

✓ Encourage the children to be aware of and take responsibility for the overall noise levels in the setting. For instance, you might have a 'noise monitor' who rings a bell when the noise levels get too high.

✓ Get the children to practise different levels of noise as a whole group – first, talking very loudly, and then talking very quietly, in turn.

✓ Give the children a good reason to keep noise levels down. For instance, you could take them outside to listen to birdsong, asking them to move really quietly so they do not scare the birds away.

✓ Have quiet times during each day when everyone gets a break from noise. Story time and show and tell are ideal for this.

✓ Create 'quiet zones' within your space where the children can go to rest and relax or to look at books quietly.

Working with families

✓ Where an individual child is being particularly noisy, this could potentially be a sign that there is some kind of hearing issue.

✓ Work with the child and their parents to explore the issue. Check that the child has had the NHS hearing test for children if you are concerned that there might be a hearing impairment.

✓ Talk with the parents about the home environment. It may be that it is noisy because of external road noise, and the child has become used to speaking loudly to be heard. It could be that there are siblings who play loud music in the house. Is there anything that can be done to mitigate this?

Case study: Biting

What's the issue?

When a child bites another child or an adult, the instinctive reaction is one of horror. However, it's actually a surprisingly common form of behaviour incident in this age group.

✓ Biting in young children is often associated with some form of distress. The child may be in pain caused by teething or may be unable to find any other way to explain how angry or frustrated they are feeling.

✓ This form of physical aggression is typically an attempt at self-soothing rather than a deliberate attack on another person.

✓ It is an issue that the vast majority of young children quickly grow out of – you do not often see older children biting their peers.

✓ Biting behaviours are a perfect example of how co-regulation with an adult can lead the child towards self-regulation.

While children will usually shrug off the incident fairly quickly, one of the key issues to deal with in this scenario is the feelings of the parents – those of both the child that was bitten and the child who bit.

Cues and clues

✓ Notice those children who are very tactile and who frequently put items in their mouth.

✓ Consider whether they are of an age where they may be in pain from teething.

✓ Keep an eye out for children who are struggling to get your attention all the time but are unable to say what they want.

✓ Look also for children who seem frustrated or angry but are unable to express what the problem is.

Strategies and solutions

✓ Stay calm and make sure that both children are well out of range of each other so that no more harm can be done. Call another member of staff over to help.

✓ Deal with the child who was bitten first, helping the child to calm down if they are still upset. Clean the bite and apply first aid as required.

✓ Talk with both children about what has happened. Ask them to describe the incident. It is best to do this separately to give them the space to express themselves.

✓ Talk to the child who bit about some alternative, more appropriate, ways to deal with their frustrations.

✓ Discuss what the child could do when they are angry. Spend plenty of time talking about this and finding alternative options.

✓ Explain to the child that teeth are for chewing and eating and not for biting.

✓ Aim to create 'three special steps' to help the child manage their anger or distress – for instance: walk away, count to five, breathe deeply.

✓ Be sure that all staff know how to handle physical incidents. Include advice on this within your behaviour management policy.

✓ Complete an incident form and talk to both sets of parents or carers when they come to pick up their children.

✓ Explain your setting policy on biting incidents to the parents and the steps that you plan to take next.

✓ Ask the child's key person to supervise them closely over the next few days and to ensure that they are not left alone with the other child.

Working with families

✓ Work with the child and their parents to try to resolve the cause of the biting and to figure out how to move forwards together.

✓ Remember that this situation is probably just as upsetting for the parents of the child who bites as it is for the parents of the child who has been bitten, because there is a lot of shame and judgement attached to this kind of behaviour.

✓ Reassure both sets of parents that you are handling the problem. Sometimes parents will ask that you exclude a child who bites. If this happens, explain that excluding the child from the setting is not an option.

✓ Ask the child's parents to come in for a meeting so that you can talk together about strategies and approaches to use if they do bite again. Check with them whether the child might be teething. Could the behaviour indicate that the child is in discomfort or distress?

✓ It's important that all practitioners in your setting react consistently if the biting happens again. Talk through your setting policy with all staff, in a staff meeting. Ensure that the child's key worker is completely clear about the steps to take and that they liaise closely with parents.

Case study: Lack of independence

What's the issue?

Helping children learn how to be independent is a tricky process, and one that can take a long time. Sometimes, a group of children will particularly struggle with this area of learning behaviours.

✓ Some children seem to need a lot of help in what should be fairly simple self-care tasks, such as putting on a coat to go outside.

✓ Similarly, some children might be in the early stages of toilet training despite being nearly at school starting age.

✓ This can be caused by a kind of 'learned helplessness', where children have been over-helped for too long.

✓ There may also be an element of nervousness around making mistakes, perhaps caused by adult reactions, or by the children feeding off subconscious 'tells' from them.

One of the key features of learning behaviour, particularly in the time leading up to starting school, is learning to become independent in self-care. In the EYFS in England, ratios change very suddenly at the start of reception, going from one adult to every eight or thirteen children to potentially one adult to thirty children.

Cues and clues

✓ Notice where children seem to rely heavily on adults to help them. Typically, the child will become very passive or even floppy when there is something that needs to be done.

✓ Consider how long it takes for children to get changed – for instance, when they go outside to play – and how much help they are given to do this. Are staff over-helping or encouraging independence?

✓ Think about how much of your setting day is taken up supporting self-care and whether this might indicate that children are not really learning to be independent.

✓ Observe the relationship between parents/carers and children at drop-off and pick-up times. You can often see clues about what is causing the issue of lack of independence at these times.

Strategies and solutions

✓ Set aside enough time for activities like getting dressed or getting changed. Learning to be independent is part of learning and does not need to be rushed. In fact, rushing can inadvertently create stress, and in doing so delay the learning.

✓ Model the process carefully for the children – for instance, this is how we put on an all-in-one suit for forest club – but also give the children space and time to have a go for themselves.

✓ Be clear with the children that making mistakes is okay – indeed, that it is to be welcomed. Talk a lot about how we can 'give it a go' even if we're not perfect at something yet.

✓ Have plenty of spare clothes so that if children do wet themselves while toilet training it is easily dealt with.

✓ Use specific and targeted praise to show the children you are pleased with their efforts to be independent.

✓ It can be helpful to set targets for children, in graduated steps – for instance, 'finding my peg' first, followed by 'getting my coat from the peg' and then 'returning it to the right peg'.

✓ Free-flow between indoors and outdoors adds a layer of challenge, but also encourages independence, because the children need to put on/take off coats, wash hands when they come back inside, and so on.

✓ A dedicated forest session is very helpful for building independence, because of the range of challenges the children face. It also requires them to regularly change into weatherproof clothing and thus improves their level of skill at this.

✓ Build in lots of opportunities to be independent through volunteering. For instance, get the children to help chop up fruit for the snacks or pass around the cups for drinks.

✓ Create an element of choice within the learning, as part of your routine, to support your children's decision-making. You might leave a space free for 'children's choice' each day, or you could have a book showing the resources on offer, and ask the children to pick out the ones they want to play with.

✓ Encourage the children to support each other in becoming more independent – for instance, helping a friend with something the friend finds hard.

Working with families

✓ Work with parents to take a consistent approach between the home and the setting. There is little point in helping to toilet train a child in your setting if parents put the child back in nappies at home and vice versa.

✓ Use setting routines to build independence, encouraging the parents and children to do as much of the 'work' at drop-off and pick-up time as you can.

✓ Encourage your families to be at home with mess as far as possible. Think about how messy it is when a baby first tries to feed. If we waited for babies to be able to do it neatly, we would be waiting a long time. Explain to parents how mess can be a positive sign.

✓ Encourage parents to send the children into your setting dressed appropriately for the challenges they will face. You don't want to be worrying that they will get paint on a lovely white designer top.

✓ There is a lot of challenge in the great outdoors, so encourage parents to take their children outdoors whenever they can.

Case study: Refusing to cooperate

What's the issue?

The opposite of cooperation is a refusal to go along with what others wish or need you to do. In some ways, it is in the job description for young children to be defiant, at least part of the time.

✓ Refusing to do what they are asked to do is all part of small children testing the boundaries that adults set for them.

✓ Young children do not perceive the world in the same way that we do as grown-ups.

✓ They don't yet really understand why it is important to put the toys away, or to eat properly, or to sit quietly and listen when someone else is talking.

✓ At this age, what we might call 'the ego' is powerfully in control. Small children often want what they want, and they want it *now*.

It is important for practitioners to differentiate between the kind of defiant behaviours that are a normal part of boundary testing and behaviours which are so severe and persistent that they might indicate some kind of SEND.

Cues and clues

✓ Some children will point-blank refuse to do something, and go floppy or rigid in order to avoid it.

✓ Sometimes practitioners become over-invested in getting children to comply. They get trapped into a position where they feel that it has become personal.

✓ Where you hear adults saying things like 'because I told you to', it is likely that there is a staff training need in terms of handling behaviours.

✓ It can be the case that staff get over-invested in pushing for cooperation when it would be better and simpler to walk away.

✓ Where you see staff demanding almost instant cooperation or compliance, this might indicate that they do not really understand the need to give children time to process instructions.

Strategies and solutions

✓ Try not to give children lots of attention when they refuse to do as you ask. Instead, focus on other children in the immediate vicinity who are doing what you need them to do.

✓ Share appropriate strategies with other staff. Make sure that everyone reacts to a refusal to cooperate in a consistent way.

✓ Remember that, if the child is not at risk in what they are doing, it is fine to simply ignore behaviours like this. Before you intervene, ask yourself what would happen if you simply ignored the child rather than responded to the refusal.

✓ Talk lots with your children about *why* it is important to be cooperative, emphasising how pleased you are when they help you do the things that need doing around the setting.

✓ Set targets and challenges to encourage all the children to help with those little 'jobs' that need doing. Make being cooperative seem playful and fun. For instance, you could ask everyone to pick up and tidy away three toys each, or to see how many red/blue/green bricks they can collect.

✓ Consider the times of day when children are most likely to refuse to cooperate in your setting. Do they tend to become difficult when they are tired?

✓ If you notice a particular pattern, consider ways to incorporate a quiet, calming activity at these times of day.

Working with families

✓ Where an individual child refuses to cooperate, talk to parents about whether they also see this behaviour at home, and if they do, how they react to it.

✓ Encourage them to use lots of positive reinforcement when the child is behaving well rather than giving the child attention when they are being difficult.

✓ Send out some WOW stickers to all your parents to encourage them to highlight positive behaviours and to catch their children behaving well.

✓ Help parents understand how to focus their attention on the *behaviour* and not on the child, as this will help them defuse any difficult behaviours. You might run a workshop on positive reinforcement and behaviour to support them.

✓ Encourage parents to be really specific with their children about *why* they are pleased with their behaviours, again to reinforce this in a positive way.

✓ Explain to parents about how attention can reinforce behaviour, either positive *or* negative. Help them see that it can be better to ignore behaviour issues and to distract rather than confront the child.

Case study: Struggling to separate

What's the issue?

It is completely normal for babies and young children to find it difficult to move from the home environment into an early years setting. Children in this age group naturally form very strong attachments to their primary carers, and this can make it tricky to move away from them.

✓ Moving to a new and unknown environment is always going to be a struggle for some (perhaps most) children.

✓ Babies and children who are not used to a range of adults being involved in their care can find this harder than those with large families or sibling groups.

✓ If children are unsettled by the transition, this can impact on their emotional wellbeing and, in turn, on their learning.

✓ Smooth transitions are therefore important to ensure good outcomes for children.

Cues and clues

✓ Where you regularly encounter issues with children settling into the setting, take a careful look at your policies around transition.

✓ If parents make 'false starts' in their child coming into your setting – perhaps trying for a week and then deciding not to send the child – this might indicate that you need to do some work in this area.

✓ Where a number of children are unsettled first thing in the morning, consider your morning routine and whether it can be enhanced.

Strategies and solutions

- ✓ Where a child is struggling to settle, ensure that the child's key person is available when they arrive at the setting.

- ✓ The key person could lead the child straight to an exciting game or resource and then sit down to play with them.

- ✓ If your setting offers the option to stay and play, take care that this does not make the transition too protracted for the parents and the child.

- ✓ Consider whether it is the parent that is experiencing emotional difficulties with the transition as well as – or rather than – the child.

- ✓ Gradually encourage parents who stay and play to move away from their own child and play with other children while they are in the setting.

- ✓ Where the child reacts negatively to this, encourage the parents to aim to ignore this rather than to engage with their own child or pay them lots of attention.

- ✓ Ask the child's key person to step in and help settle the child so that they get used to receiving emotional support from another adult.

Where children and parents are really anxious, it can help to gradually increase the time the child spends alone at the setting – perhaps just half an hour at first. The parent should be clear with the child that they are leaving rather than trying to leave without the child realising, so that the child knows they will not be abandoned without warning. The parent should say that they will be back soon, but once they have done this, they should exit decisively to make a clean break.

Working with families

- ✓ Encourage parents to walk or drive past your setting before the child actually starts with you, to gradually get them used to where the setting is and what it looks like.

- ✓ Share images of the setting during the home visit so that it feels more familiar to the child when they start with you.

✓ Remember that parents can subconsciously transmit their own anxieties to the child, so focus on supporting and easing the fears of both the child and the parents.

✓ It can sometimes help if the child can be dropped off by a different known adult – for instance, a grandparent – so that the separation is slightly less discomforting for them.

✓ Encourage the child's parents to send in a 'show and tell' toy, or a favourite cuddly, as a link to the home environment while they are at the setting.

Case study: Physically aggressive behaviours

What's the issue?

It is always distressing to see a young child lash out and use physical aggression, whether this is against other children or against staff. There can be a lot of emotion involved in a situation where a child has hurt someone, because it can feel extremely personal to the person who has been hurt.

✓ These kinds of behaviours will often indicate that the child has an inability to communicate their frustrations.

✓ The child cannot express what the problem is, or control their emotional reactions, and so they lash out in a physical manner.

✓ Children who are physically aggressive need to learn how to handle their own emotions and also how to socialise with others.

✓ It is vital that children learn these skills before they move on to the more formal environment of the later school years.

✓ Remember that the process of learning how to play with others, and how to handle our emotions when we don't get what we want, is a normal part of early child development.

Cues and clues

✓ Some children very quickly become physical when their desires are frustrated.

✓ Physical outbursts can be a signal of levels of over-excitement that the child is unable to bring under control.

✓ The atmosphere in the setting appears to become too heightened for certain children at certain times.

✓ Sometimes a child will lash out at one particular peer, perhaps in a misguided attempt to befriend them and get their attention.

Strategies and solutions

✓ As a staff, agree a clear and consistent reaction for when a child behaves in an aggressive way.

✓ Staff should lead the child calmly away from the situation and take them somewhere quiet to calm down. Once they are calm, they can then have a chat and think about what happened.

✓ Where the child refuses to move, staff should ask the other children to move away from them, in order to defuse the situation.

✓ When talking to the child, remember to refer to the behaviour as the problem rather than the child. Use phrases that depersonalise the situation – for instance, saying, 'That behaviour is not okay' rather than 'You were very naughty.'

✓ Once the child has calmed down, get them to consider how other children feel when the physically aggressive behaviour happens. Encourage them to develop empathy by talking with them about what they think other children might be feeling.

✓ Talk with the child about what happened in the run-up to the outburst. Was there a trigger for the behaviour that you can identify together?

✓ You might try modelling some situations where the trigger happens and showing the child how they might deal with it in a different way.

✓ Look for some really positive physical outlets for the child to help them deal with their frustrations – for instance, bouncing a basketball or pummelling a cushion.

Working with families

✓ Talk with the parents about whether they have seen similar behaviours at home.

✓ Are they able to identify the antecedents for this behaviour? What is happening just before the outbursts?

✓ Have a chat about whether the child is getting enough physical outlets at home. How much time do they spend playing, getting exercise or going outdoors?

✓ You could suggest some suitable options for the child to get rid of any excess energy and physicality outside of the setting.

Case study: Destructive behaviours

It has been said that the opposite of creative behaviour is destructive behaviour – the desire to destroy for no apparent purpose. A lot of what appears to be deliberately destructive behaviour in children can be traced back to frustrations or to some kind of developmental need.

What's the issue?

✓ Some children will behave towards their environment in a way that is negative or destructive.

✓ This might manifest itself in behaviours such as damaging resources, scribbling on walls, racing around the space and knocking into things.

✓ Parents and practitioners can find these behaviours distressing because of the value that we put on the places where we live and work.

✓ The destructive behaviours can appear to feel cathartic for the child – a way of getting rid of excess energy.

Cues and clues

✓ Children move from one area of the setting to another without ever settling to one activity for any prolonged period of time.

✓ Your setting feels unnecessarily untidy at the end of the day, with lots of toys and resources scattered everywhere.

✓ You spend a lot of time tidying up after children and cleaning up spillages.

✓ Resources and toys are regularly damaged and have to be replaced.

✓ Staff seem very frayed at the end of the day and become snappy with each other. The children's behaviours seem to be filtering through to staff relationships.

Strategies and solutions

✓ Think about whether the behaviours might arise from something to do with the way that you are setting up the provision. Is there simply so much out for the children to play with that the temptation to mess about with it has become overwhelming?

✓ Consider whether you need to see the apparently destructive behaviours as a 'problem' or whether you could channel them into something different.

✓ Think about what the child is trying to 'tell' you when they perform these behaviours. Are they saying something to you about the way that they would like to learn? Is there a schema going on that you might notice and that would help you make sense of what appear to be destructive behaviours? For instance, where a child repeatedly scribbles on the walls, this could simply be the sign of an urge to do more mark making. Perhaps you could designate an area where the children can mark make directly onto large sheets of paper or wallpaper stuck onto the walls.

✓ Similarly, the child who constantly tips toys out of boxes might actually be looking for more boxes to play with, or to get inside the boxes, rather than deliberately making a mess. Perhaps the child has an enclosing or trajectory schema?

✓ The child's key person could spend some time observing them before staff talk together as a team about what has been observed.

✓ Consider what learning needs the child has, and what next steps you could focus on as a team. How might you channel the behaviours into more creative outcomes?

✓ Set up situations where the child can use their desires in more productive ways – for instance, challenge the child to count ten items out of or into a box rather than just tipping the whole lot out.

✓ Create opportunities for the child to perform the behaviours that are being repeated (e.g. tipping/scribbling) in a way that is productive rather than destructive – for instance, tipping water from one jug into another or scribbling on long sheets of paper outdoors.

✓ Talk to the child about why it might not be appropriate to behave like this. Ask the child what the problems might be with their behaviours – for instance, someone could trip over toys left on the floor, or the toys might get damaged.

Working with families

✓ Talk to the parents about what is going on. Have they noticed similar behaviours at home? What strategies have they used to deal with these situations?

✓ Aim to agree on a consistent approach at home and in the setting to avoid any confusion for the child.

✓ Give the parents suggestions about ways to allow the child to find a physical outlet for these urges that is not problematic – for instance, shredding paper or scribbling on a patio using outdoor chalks.

✓ Ask the parents to highlight and reinforce the times when the child is creative rather than destructive – you might ask them to fill out some WOW slips that you can add to the child's learning journey or display in the setting.

Conclusion

My hope is that the advice and ideas in this book will help all my readers support their children in building the skill of self-regulation. The work that early years educators do forms the bedrock for all that happens later on in a child's education, and there is probably no more important element of this work than helping children learn how to control their own behaviours and their own learning.

It has been a pleasure and a privilege to work in the sector for the last decade, alongside a passionate and dedicated workforce who do so much for the children in their settings.

I wish all my readers well with their work in the early years, and hope that they enjoy the time they spend supporting their children as they play, grow, develop and carry on learning behaviours.

Endnotes

Chapter 3

1. John Hattie (2009). *Visible Learning: A synthesis of over 800 meta-analyses related to achievement.* Abingdon: Routledge. Carol Dweck (2017). *Mindset: Changing the way you think to fulfil your potential* (updated edition). London: Robinson.

Chapter 4

2. You can find a useful short guide to executive function here: https://developingchild.harvard.edu/guide/a-guide-to-executive-function/.

3. See, for example, Chaiklin, S. The zone of proximal development in Vygotsky's analysis of learning and instruction, http://blogs.ubc.ca/vygotsky/files/2013/11/chaiklin.zpd_.pdf.

Chapter 5

4. Ann Clare provides an explanation of this concept in her blog post "'Professional Love" in Early Years Settings' on the Professional Association for Childcare and Early Years (PACEY) website. See https://www.pacey.org.uk/news-and-views/pacey-blog/2016/july-2016/%E2%80%98professional-love%E2%80%99-in-early-years-settings/.

Chapter 6

5. See https://www.unicef.org.uk/what-we-do/un-convention-child-rights/.

6. Fisher, J. (2016). *Interacting or Interfering: Improving interactions in the early years.* Maidenhead: Open University Press.

Chapter 7

7. See Ofsted (2019). *Education inspection framework: Overview of research*, p. 15, https://assets.publishing.service.gov.uk/government/uploads/system/uploads/attachment_data/file/926364/Research_for_EIF_framework_100619__16_.pdf.

8. See, for example, Csíkszentmihályi, M. (1998). *Finding Flow: The psychology of engagement with everyday life*. New York, NY: Basic Books.

9. For descriptions of different types of schema, see the PACEY website at https://www.pacey.org.uk/working-in-childcare/spotlight-on/schemas/ and Arnerich, M. (2019). How to identify schemas in play: A powerful tool for any early years practitioner (Cathy Nutbrown interview), *Famly* (blog), https://famly.co/blog/management/identify-schemas-in-play-cathy-nutbrown/.

Chapter 8

10. Strong-Wilson, T. and Ellis, J. (2007). Children and Place: Reggio Emilia's environment as third teacher, *Theory into Practice*, 46(1), pp. 40–47.

11. See https://elizabethjarman.com/.